D1519316

The Early Poetry of W. B. Yeats

Kennikat Press
National University Publications
Literary Criticism Series

General Editor
John E. Becker
Fairleigh Dickinson University

THE EARLY POETRY OF
W. B. YEATS

The Poetic Quest

THOMAS L. BYRD, JR.

National University Publications
KENNIKAT PRESS // 1978
Port Washington, N.Y. // London

90275

Manufactured in the United States of America

Published by
Kennikat Press Corp.
Port Washington, N.Y./London

Library of Congress Cataloging in Publication Data

Byrd, Thomas L
    The early poetry of W. B. Yeats.

    (Literary criticism series) (National university publications)
    Bibliography: p.
    Includes index.
    1. Yeats, William Butler, 1865–1939—Criticism and interpretation. I. Title.
PR5907.B9   921'.8   77-2576
ISBN 0-8046-9184-3

TO DOMINIQUE

CONTENTS

The Early Poetry of W. B. Yeats

ABOUT THE AUTHOR

Thomas L. Byrd taught English and humanities at the
University of Florida and lectured at Loyola University's
Rome Center of Liberal Arts. He is now lecturing at the
Faculté Catholique de Lille, teaching at the Institut de
Formation Pédagogique et Psychosociologique in Paris, and is
Directeur Pédagogique of the Centre International de
Formation in Paris.

Professor Byrd received his bachelor's degree from Emory
University, and studied at Harvard before earning his master's
degree from Brown University and his doctorate from the
University of Florida.

A native of Atlanta, he has had a long and abiding interest
in Yeats, which has been furthered by travel through the
West of Ireland. As a result, work on this book was appropriately
begun in County Sligo.

INTRODUCTION

The main purpose of this book is to discuss, in a clear and un-
pedantic manner, some important aspects of the early poetry of
W. B. Yeats. When the work behind this book was begun, the
primary aim was to gain a reasonable and sound perspective on
the early poetry of Yeats. Lately, this original purpose seems, if
it is possible, even more valid and necessary. In recent years,
many scholarly studies have appeared on the subject of Yeats:
valuable insights are contained in these works, to be sure, and
the Early Yeats has definitely been "rediscovered."

This study, however, attempts to examine the early poetry
without yielding to the temptation to inflate it beyond its actual
worth and, at the same time, to avoid obscuring its true nature
in the critical process. This book, therefore, is not an examina-
tion of recent trends in Yeatsian criticism. It is, rather, a parallel
examination of the early poetry of Yeats from a different per-
spective and from a different critical philosophy.

The reader of Yeats is often confused or even deterred by the
very complexity of the poet and of his commentators. The "Yeats-
ians," as students of Yeats are sometimes called, are all too often
treated as members of a select group possessing a body of arcane
knowledge from which the "average" reader of poetry is sum-
marily excluded. These comments, it should be added, are not
intended to imply that Yeats is easy; they are meant to encour-
age, and ultimately to reveal some insights that will, hopefully,
add to the reader's perception and understanding.

Yeats has often enough been seen as the dilettante, the dabbler in esoterica, the young man obsessed by the command "Hammer your thoughts into unity" but unable to act upon it. The early Yeats has also been seen by Graham Hough as the last of the Romantics, by Arthur Symons as the foremost practitioner of Symbolism in English, by himself as a poet "in all things Pre-Raphaelite."[1] Fortunately some critics (even in the 1960s—Balachandra Rajan and Donald Davie, for example) have realized that the early Yeats cannot be conveniently labeled and that a definite break or turning point in Yeats's poetry cannot be found as conveniently as it was formerly supposed.[2] I take the position here that Yeats is, in part, a Romantic, a Symbolist, a Pre-Raphaelite, and perhaps a mystic. Much of his poetry falls into another important tradition, the Pastoral. This study will concentrate upon Yeats's very personal adaptation of the pastoral genre and an important theme or set of metaphors that not only is included in the pastoral but also serves to unify the early poetry: the figure of the poet-seeker and the poetic quest for truth.

The poet-seeker gives to Yeats's poetry a definite unity and coherence. Of course, this theme is not the only underlying concept in Yeats, nor does it at all times overshadow other major themes and ideas. It does constitute, nonetheless, a striking pattern, and it provides an added dimension to a reading of the poetry and some of the plays.

The seeker after truth appears throughout world literature, from Homer to the present day. The search for truth and reality and the problems surrounding the very use of words in the process of the quest are of primary concern to the serious writer. The difficulty is not merely one of communication, nor is it limited to the validity of various poetic or literary devices: it becomes, ultimately, a metaphysical question. Extreme manifestations of this concern can be seen in the works of Gertrude Stein and Samuel Beckett, to name only two of the experimentalists who have carried language to its ultimate extreme—the attempt to transcend language and its limitations. The lack of a common mythology, a common frame of reference, has led to much of the disillusion of the late nineteenth century, and the first seven decades of the twentieth. One has only to consider the "Art for

Art's Sake" movement and the ephemeral nature of art and "non-art" forms that arise briefly to see clearly the problems that face the modern artist. From about 1880 to the present time, all forms of art have been pervaded by a cynicism that often borders on despair, with the exception of a few major figures such as Yeats and Picasso, both of whom were willing to experiment and change, and a few bursts of enthusiasm such as those of the 1920s and the 1960s, and even within these periods of creation, one can see a world of art that combines excitement with negativism and that is dominated by an atmosphere of impermanence.

One reason for what has been called the "permanence of Yeats" is that he did not despair of the use of words (though one must examine his *Plays for Dancers,* written for masked and silent dancers). Another reason is that he searched for a mythology (or mythologies) that, if not common to all, would be congenial to himself and would contain a freshness not found in the "standard" myths of Greece and Rome. Yeats's myths became both personal and nationalistic, but not incomprehensible for the educated reader willing to give poetry the study it deserves. Yeats remained within the common stream of English literature by writing in English; he never learned Gaelic and thus was never drawn into an insular form of total nationalism. His poetry is for the world, not just for Ireland. Like William Faulkner, he writes about his homeland but he deals with themes that transcend the borders of region, nation, and time.

In the final analysis, the concern here is with Yeats's own approach to the search for reality and truth. In studying Yeats's poetry from the earliest writings through the later works, it becomes apparent that Yeats is concerned with this quest throughout his career. In the very earliest poetry, in works some scholars wish he had never written, before Yeats found his true voice in his native Ireland, the search is already a major theme. Since many of these poems are neglected by scholars who find themselves embarrassed by works that are less than mature, and because some of these poems are left out of the definitive edition, there will be an emphasis here on the juvenilia as well as some of the more familiar poems. The early verse dramas, *The Island of Statues* and *The Seeker,* are stressed because, surprisingly enough, they can be seen as seeds from which the later poems germinate. In actuality, Yeats is not one of the "last Romantics": he is a modern Romantic. In the early poetry there are, to be sure, many affinities with the nineteenth century, which, considering the dates of the poems, is only to be expected. However, although much of the poetry to be discussed here was written in the nineteenth century, it is not merely the product of its age. It is neither the voice of the old century nor the prelude to the new. In these works, Yeats reveals his development as a unique artist whose genesis should not be ignored.

By concentrating on the early poetry, I do not mean to imply that Yeats is, as it were, an artistic schizophrenic. The later poetry should always be kept in mind: I am not writing from the point of view that it does not or should not exist. It is quite valid, and often necessary, to see the earlier poetry as the initiatory step of the beginning poet in a development that culminates in the mature vision of the later poems. The focus will be, however, upon the early poems and poetic dramas—for convenience, those written in or before 1906—in order to stress not just their importance to the later poetry, but their value in their own right. The tendency of many readers to examine the early poetry merely as a prelude to the poems of the 1914 and subsequent volumes, creates but vague thoughts couched in beautiful language. They are not, as Norman Jeffares observed in a talk for Radio Eireann, "impersonal love poetry, sad, melancholic, weak . . . abstracted from life and languished in vague mists of affirmation, of ideal beauty and ideal Ireland."[3] The poetry written between 1885 and 1906, even including much of the very early work omitted from the definitive edition, reveals a profound and continuing artistic and philosophical concern that places Yeats among the major poets of the nineteenth century. It is not enough to say that without these earlier poems such later works as "Byzantium" would never have been written, though it is true that, throughout this period, Byzantium is always in the distance.

I have stated above that Yeats is "perhaps a mystic." The qualification does not indicate critical timidity. There is a strong temptation in dealing with Yeats to label him a mystic of some sort and then happily hedge around the problem created by that term by discussing his association with such organizations as the

Hermetical Society of the Golden Dawn, his interest in Blake, his discussion of Shelley's symbols, and his own use of symbols. Rather than confuse the issue, it is wiser to say that Yeats is a seeker of spiritual wisdom, and that his search emerges in his poetry, among other ways, in the theme of the wanderer-seeker and his quest for poetic wisdom.

At this point another temptation enters—biography. Yeats's personal life may seem important, for there too he was continually searching for spiritual wisdom. However, lengthy biographical discussion is often more confusing than helpful. It is sufficient to note that Yeats's personal search took many forms, and that the exact goal of the search was often vague or ambiguous. One need only look at his comments about *A Vision:* Is it a system in which he believed, or is it "metaphors for poetry"? We may never know. In general, though, the many paths of Yeats's own search and the illusory goal parallel the same elements in the poetry.

It is in this connection that the pastoral tradition, in its more modern conception, is particularly illuminating in understanding Yeats, since it provides a framework or pattern for the search. This concept of pastoral specifies that the shepherd is other than or more than a shepherd. Eleanor Terry Lincoln, in her introduction to *Pastoral and Romance,* states that the shepherd is "a musician, a poet, a prince, and a priest." The shepherd withdraws from the world to a "place apart" in order to gain insight into the world of man; he then returns with his new knowledge to engage in active life. The shepherd does not escape: the universe of the pastoral has elements of Eden, but it is definitely post-Edenic.[4] To avoid the Judaeo-Christian terminology, one could say that the shepherd is similar to a bodhisattva, or one near that state of spiritual development, whose knowledge and enlightenment is gained in retirement but who chooses to be bound to the world. It should be mentioned that in Yeats the pattern is rarely this clearcut. For reasons that will become evident, an ambiguity and uncertainty hovers over much of the poetry. In dealing with the early poetry from this point of view, the greater part of this discussion will be in what T. R. Henn calls "that indeterminate country where the metaphor becomes a symbol."[5] This is the country of meditation, vision, and dream, in which values shift as the poet studies many facets of his art and thought. It is the area of the Celtic Twilight, a term that has wrongly repelled too many readers, for the Celtic Twilight is itself a metaphor for the poetic dream, an ambiguous state described by Yeats in the notes to *The Wind Among the Reeds:*

> I had sometimes when awake, but more often in sleep, moments of vision, a state very unlike dreaming, when these images took upon themselves what seemed an independent life and became part of a mystic language, which always seemed as if it would bring me some strange revelation.[6]

Directly involved in an understanding of Yeats's use of symbol is the true meaning to Yeats of the dream. The word *dream* does not have the respectability of *vision*. A vision is living, and it has a certain established place in the world of the spirit. A dream, however, is somehow a fake, and a lethargic fake at that. We see no active contemplation in the act of dreaming. Yet Yeats did feel that dreams are important, and not only in a Freudian sense. A dream is one link between the world of daily life and the unseen world of the spirit. Dreams come to all people, not just to a favored few; thus the dream becomes a universal point of reference that all can understand. A symbol seen in a dream will more often than not be cloudy to the conscious mind, yet it is real nonetheless. In order to understand at least in part that which is unseen, we are forced to see through a glass darkly, or not see at all.

Norman Jeffares objects that Yeats's early poems lack the "honesty" of the later verses and that Yeats deliberately attempts to conceal the full meaning in his early symbolism and his "vague and often unsuitable notes."[7] What Mr. Jeffares does not seem to recognize is that in the earlier poetry Yeats is using a type of symbolism closely akin to, but not identical with, that of the French Symbolists: Yeats is not working toward an exact objective correlative; he does not want his symbols to be specifically concrete. His symbols are suggestive, and often suggestive in a cumulative effect. The rose, for example, is not derived from any specific source. Yeats was pleased to find it in many places, ranging from Irish poetry to Rosicrucianism, but he was not restricted by any particular use of the rose outside of his own poetry. For Yeats, the rose could refer to Ireland, Maud Gonne,

love in general, intellectual beauty, higher truth, mystical truth
—or any or all of these. The rose is an idealized symbol suggest-
ing warmth, sensuous softness, color, intellectual beauty, and
Ireland; and any attempt to limit it destroys its evocations and
suggestions: thus the vague notes to which Mr. Jeffares objects.

Yeats's comments on his reactions to reading *Axel* before his
trip to Paris in 1894 are helpful in understanding his own reac-
tions to symbols:

It did not move me because I thought it a great masterpiece, but because
it seemed part of a religious rite, the ceremony perhaps of some secret
order wherein my generation had been initiated. Even those strange sen-
tences so much in the manner of my time—"as to living, our servants will
do that for us": "O to veil you with my hair where you will breathe the
spirit of dead roses"—did not seem so important as the symbols: the forest
castle, the treasure, the lamp that burned before Solomon.[8]

The symbols that appealed to Yeats in *Axel* are quite similar to
many symbols found in his own poetry—objects and references
that evoke a larger meaning, and often an arcane meaning hidden
in part even to the poet himself. Yeats's symbols are the symbols
of the search, not of a goal already reached. Yeats was involved
in the poetic world discussed by Arthur Symons in *The Symbol-
ist Movement in Literature,* a world in the process of being
mapped and explored, but not a world permeated with the
self-confidence of recent discovery or the cynicism of delusion.
Symons looks for "the turn of the soul," after which will come
"a literature in which the visible world is no longer a reality,
and the unseen world no longer a dream."[9]

Yeats has constructed a total poetic universe, a microcosm in
which the poet can exist and that gives focus and positive meaning
to his ideas, themes, and philosophy. Yeats's poetic quest is not
an escape from reality, but a search for the true reality, for the
valid microcosm—the world in which he can express his thought
coherently, a small world that, by analogy, becomes a total sym-
bol for the entire realm of human experience. Herein lies the
value of Yeats's studies in mythological correspondences and
correlations, his searches into various religious systems and philos-
ophies. Herein also lies the true significance of his obsession with
the phrase "Hammer your thoughts into unity." He had to prove

for himself that the microcosm that became true for him, ancient and modern Ireland (Sligo and Galway in particular), could provide not only a particular milieu for his own thought but also a symbolic milieu in which that thought would assume a universal relevance.

THE ENVIRONMENT OF THE QUEST

THE POETIC DREAM

The pastoral world and Yeats's poetic dream are very closely allied in that they are both a "place apart," and they combine to form the environment of the poetic quest. It will be domonstrated later that Yeats's pastoral world, no matter how artificial it may seem on the surface, is invariably allied with the world of everyday life by such means as the use of ordinary creatures and objects of nature; by reference, allusion, or their physical presence, Yeats makes sure that the small, familiar things of daily life are not forgotten.

Yeats does not operate on a theory of correspondences in which the "other world" must be described in terms of "this world" because the world in which we live is all we see and know. He is, rather, describing a universe in which two worlds are really one world. Man, through civilization, has lost the capacity to see the "other world," which is, in actuality, all around him. It takes a person like the seer or the relatively uncivilized peasant to comprehend the truth that the world of immortal creatures (such as the fairies) and the world of mortal creatures are really one and the same. In a sense, a third world, that of the past, is also directly involved in the world of the present. A science-fiction story might treat Yeats's view of the universe in the form of a fourth dimension, but for Yeats the barrier that exists for us is a purely artificial one created by modern culture. Even though the beings that inhabit the "two worlds" are different in

such respects as mortality and immortality, they are not separated
by a barrier that is part of the structure of the cosmos.

The dream becomes one means of breaking through the artifi-
cial barrier. In the world of the dream, the barrier can cease to
exist: the symbols seen in dreams often come from and connect
us with both the "past" and the "supernatural." Through these
symbols, all becomes "natural" and "real." Yeats's dream assumes
a certain mystical aura: it becomes a moment or state of enlight-
enment. Yeats observes, in *Plays for an Irish Theatre:*

> Tragic art, passionate art, moves us by setting us to reverie, by alluring us
> almost to the intensity of trance. . . . This reverie, this twilight between
> sleep and waking, is the condition of tragic pleasure.

Professor F. A. C. Wilson, in *W. B. Yeats and Tradition,* concludes
from this statement that Yeats demands from the theatre not
catharsis but "a single moment of emotional equipoise to which
all the passionate intensity of the action will tend . . . a moment
when the mind passes through profound emotion into a condi-
tion of absolute calm."[10] Although these comments are specifically
related to drama, they have an equally valid application to the
poetry, especially since Yeats was particularly aware that drama
is a form of poetry; both are valued in the oral tradition and thus
help us to regain the frame of reference in which the "super-
stitious" peasant lives, where the spoken word transmitted
through the ages of man, or composed in the present, has power
and truth.[11] In the verse as well as the plays, Yeats sees a truth
in dreams, and this truth is a valid and essential part of his poetic
search. To cite only a few examples, in "Fergus and the Druid,"
Fergus wishes to learn from the Druid "the dreaming wisdom
that is yours" (l. 22). In "The Hosting of the Sidhe," Niamh
calls, "Empty your heart of its mortal dream" (l. 5), a definite
contrast of mortal with immortal. In "The Withering of the
Boughs," a poem first published in 1900, the refrain states:

> No boughs have withered because of the wintry wind;
> The boughs have withered because I have told them my dreams.

In these three poems we see two of the most important attri-
butes of dreaming in the poetry of Yeats: wisdom and power.

In "Fergus and the Druid," the Druid possesses a wisdom that
for Fergus is more desirable than an earthly kingdom. The re-
lationship of the earthly state to the spiritual contains an ambi-
guity that Fergus wishes to transcend:

> A king is but a foolish labourer
> Who wastes his blood to be another's dream.
>   (ll. 27-28)

When Fergus gains the bag of dreams from the Druid, and has
known the wisdom, he reflects:

> And all these things were wonderful and great;
> But now I have grown nothing, knowing all.
>   (ll. 37-38)

In "The Withering of the Boughs," the power of the dream is self-
evident in the refrain quoted above. The dream, and not the
power of the elements of nature, has withered the boughs. In
this poem the wisdom gives meaning to the power. The persona
has knowledge of both worlds: of the moon "murmuring to the
birds" (l. 1) of "the isles where the Danaan kind / Wind and un-
wind their dances when the light grows cool" (ll. 12-13, 1900
version), of "the sleepy country" where a king and queen are
wandering "so deaf and so blind / With wisdom. . . " (ll. 17-21),
and "the curlew and peewit on Echtge of streams" (l. 22), where
he falls asleep, dreaming.

In "The Hosting of the Sidhe," the type of dream assumes an
importance, the same importance implied in a statement by
Lady Gregory: "As Mr. Yeats puts it, the countryman's 'dream
has never been entangled by reality.' "[12] In the context of Yeats's
writings, "mortal dream" and "reality" probably have a close
kinship, but not an identity. The mortal dream is not condemned,
but there is a taint on the word reality here. The problem seems
to be one of true and false reality; and the answer has not been
found. Fergus as king is a dream to others; yet he is unhappy
being this dream and seeks the dream of the Druid. When he has
the dream of the Druid, he is again unhappy, but in the compan-
ion poem "Who Goes with Fergus?" the dream of Fergus the poet
becomes the object of quest. Fergus, with the knowledge and

power of the Druid, has now become a symbol in the same way
in which the Druid is a symbol. He is, in this sense, an object
beckoning from afar. Of course, happiness and wisdom do not
necessarily go hand in hand. In *The Island of Statues,* Naschina
repeatedly asks the Enchantress, "But art thou happy?" After
a series of evasions, she replies: "Youth, I am at peace" (II, iii,
ll. 144–159). The question of peace and happiness, rest and mo-
tion in the quest of the poet will be discussed in greater detail
later. It is sufficient here to mention that there is an uneasiness
involved in the dream, that the act of dreaming or the attainment
of a "higher" dream does not necessarily indicate the culmina-
tion of a search, and that the dreamer does not necessarily reach
a state of tranquillity. One is reminded of the ecstasy reached by
Shelley, which involved supreme pleasure and pain, or the states
of mind attained by Keats in "Ode to a Nightingale," which in-
clude drugged pain, longing, confusion, and bewilderment.

There is much more to the dream in Yeats than reverie: Yeats's
dreams exist on a number of levels. There is a relativity involved
that cannot be reduced to a formula. The wisdom of the dream
is sought from two totally different types of persons, the first
represented by a figure such as the Druid, the second by the
countryman or the unlettered peasant. Dreaming wisdom is to be
found in the esoteric mysticism possessed by the Druid or in the
intuitive simplicity of the peasant. Both are essential to an under-
standing of Yeats, and an overemphasis on either produces a
fatal distortion to the total meaning of the dream in Yeats's
poetry.

Much has been written about Yeats's mysticism. Morton Seiden
states that "by identifying literary theory and nature myth with
white magic, he [Yeats] wrote of Orphic priests, Gaelic druids,
Irish bards, folk minstrels, magi, spiritualists, and nineteenth-
century symbolist poets as though there were no differences
among them."[13] Historically, of course, there were vast differ-
ences among them, but Yeats saw in them one basic and essential
similarity—they were all seekers of and interpreters of the hidden
spiritual truths of the universe. It is for this same reason that
Yeats was fascinated in real life by such persons as Madame
Blavatsky (who claimed direct wisdom from the eternal Masters),
Mohini Chatterjee, and servants and peasants in County Sligo

and County Galway. All these (and others) had seen, or claimed to have seen, the spiritual side of the universe that is hidden to the man too involved in the cares of the world and in urban life. As far as an understanding of Yeats's poetry is concerned, a discourse on what is known (or guessed) about the Orphic mysteries or Druidism would be of little help, since the importance of these elements in the poetry is not scholarly but symbolic. They suggest ancient and hidden mysteries known to men of old and to the man who has not lost touch with the totality of the universe around him, but forgotten by modern man in the hustling materialism of the industrial world. The Druid, then, becomes a suggestive symbol, representative of an almost lost but essential facet of the human condition. The Druid, or, in a more general sense, the mystic wise with the lore of the centuries, is a part of true reality; the peasant and the land of the peasants are countercomponents in which this reality can be sought.

Herein lies the true significance of the Irish landscape in Yeats, for the dream and the land are vitally connected with each other. The land is the home of the peasant; it is the locale in which the ancient ways still live. The Irish poetry becomes a turning point in the poetic search. Concerning Yeats's finest and probably most famous "Irish" poem, "The Lake Isle of Innisfree," Louis MacNeice states that it is not, as Stephen Spender says, "A poem which 'calls up the image of a young man reclining on a yellow satin sofa'"; rather, it is "a protest against London" and "an escape to a real place in Ireland which represented to him certain Irish realities."[14] MacNeice's quite valid statement supports the idea that Yeats is using the West of Ireland in the true sense of pastoral: if the word *escape* is to be applied to Yeats at all, it must be used in the context of an escape *from* London and all the metropolis represents, and an escape *to* the true realities found in more remote, less industrialized areas.

Yeats's use of the County Sligo and County Galway landscapes in the early poetry is not an affectation or a part of a vague fin-de-siècle nostalgia for the rustic. If the specific places—Sleuth Wood, Glen-Car, Innisfree, and the like—are compared with the earlier Arcadian and Indian landscapes or with the other-world landscapes seen by Oisin in his wanderings, the Irish countryside emerges as a concrete metaphor for that unity of being that Yeats

sought all his life. In Ireland, Yeats tells us again and again, in
poetry and prose, the physical and the spiritual worlds are direct-
ly linked, as the old peasant tales attest: at Rosses Point, if one
happens to fall asleep on the rocks, his soul is likely to be stolen
by the fairies; there is a door in the side of Ben Bulben connect-
ing the underworld land of faerie with the upper world of man;
the burial cairn of the prehistorical Queen Maeve dominates the
countryside around Sligo. The supernatural and the legendary
past are visibly present and directly inform the atmosphere of
the area. Man lives not just among hills, trees, lakes, and the
ocean—he lives in the totality of the universe, the physical and
the spiritual, the present and the past. In Yeats's early poetry—as
indeed it is later—the very environment of man is taken for ex-
actly what it is; not what it should be, as in a self-conscious
idealization, nor as man has made it to be, as in a planned suburb
or the clean ordered setting of St. James's Park. Though Yeats
does not, of course, describe in a strictly photographic manner,
his Irish landscapes are remarkably true to the actual places, far
more so than the landscapes in Arnold, Tennyson, or even Words-
worth, who is more realisitic in his descriptions than is often
realized. For example, on Innisfree there is room for a tiny cot-
tage, nine bean rows, and very little else. The landscape is not
romanticized, and it is not merely a setting for greater things:
man lives in and through the world around him, and the world
becomes more than a metaphor. The microcosm *is* the macrocosm.
The peasant, of course, is already aware of this relationship. The
modern man must search for it. Yeats sought through Arcadia
and India until he realized, as he expressed it later, that "Ancient
Ireland knew it all." This statement, however, is from Yeats's
last poem, "Under Ben Bulben." In the early poetry, though
Yeats seems convinced that the spiritual and the physical worlds
are directly linked, that one can connect with the other, that
a man can stand in a crowd in the small, grey village of Dromo-
hair and dream of fairyland, he is still searching for the true
meaning and unity of the relationship of the two worlds. The
physical and the spiritual coexist not in a four-dimensional sense
but actually in three dimensions, if one can only become aware
of this truth—the truth "civilization" has obscured for us.
    When Yeats localized his search in the landscape of Ireland, he

gave to his poetry a quality that increased his depth, richness, and universality of appeal. One could venture to say that without this quality (which is directly related to that which the Abbey Players came to call irreverently "P. Q."–peasant quality) Yeats could never have become as great a poet as he is. As we shall see later, such poems as "The Lake Isle of Innisfree" have a much deeper significance than the Arcadian and Indian poems because of their direct relationship to specific geographical locations.

Yeats weaves his landscapes into the same tapestry with Cuchulain, Oisin, Maud Gonne, and Helen of Troy. The Ireland of Oisin is still here, in the same way that Maud Gonne is another Helen. The ancient Helen gains immediacy while the modern Maud Gonne gains historicity. The historical moment and the present become juxtaposed and fused into unity. Though much has been made of Yeats's concept of the cyclic nature of time, and his use of the gyre, in one sense past and present can be said to exist simultaneously. We cannot say that Maud Gonne is a reincarnation of Helen, nor that they are the same person, but we do see both of them as though we were viewing them from the timelessness of eternity. Confusion results when the reader cannot escape, even partially, from the temporal view of existence.

In this sense, Dorothy Hoare is wrong, in her discussion of *The Works of Morris and of Yeats in Relation to Early Saga Literature,* when she concludes that Yeats withdraws from real life into "the shadows of ancestral memory" through contemplation of ancient heroic life.[15] It is true, as she states, that the sagas represent an ideal–but, for Yeats, the ideal has not been lost. To Yeats the "shadows of ancestral memory" were not shadows at all: they were a definite and an integral part of reality, a part that had been lost in the rush of civilization in the cities but had been retained in the countryside of the West of Ireland. Even in his later life, Coole Park and the tower that he purchased as a home were significant to him because of their associations with the noble past, associations that were even more important because of the physical existence of these places in the present. Unlike the Pre-Raphaelite group in London, Yeats did not try to reconstruct the past in the way in which he wished it had existed. He found it already existing in the present.

Norman Jeffares has observed that "there is a division to be made between poems which draw upon the Celtic legends and those which owe their inspiration to localized memories of places."[16] However, if this division is made, the significance of both groups of poems becomes lessened, for the places add meaning to the legends, and the legends often are a vital part of the places. Also, quite significantly, some poems, such as "The Hosting of the Sidhe," combine both legend and place:

> The host is riding from Knocknarea
> And over the grave of Clooth-na-Bare;
> Caoilte tossing his burning hair,
> And Niamh calling *Away, come away*.
>   (ll. 1–4)

The legends clustered around such places as Knocknarea, the mountain on which the burial cairn of Queen Maeve is located, are not bits of esoterica gleaned from the museum, but part of the living reality of the place. The mystical importance of the landscape to Yeats is clearly seen in this passage from the first draft of the Autobiography, which has been transcribed and edited by Denis Donoghue:

An obsession more constant than anything but my love itself was the need of mystical rites—a ritual system of evocation and meditation—to reunite the perception of the spirit, of the divine, with natural beauty. I believed that instead of thinking of Judea as holy we should [think] our own land holy, and most holy where most beautiful. Commerce and manufacture had made the world ugly; the death of pagan nature-worship had robbed visible beauty of its inviolable sanctity. I was convinced that all lonely and lovely places were crowded with invisible beings and that it would be possible to communicate with them. I meant to initiate young men and women in this worship, which would unite the radical truths of Christianity to those of a more ancient world, and to use the Castle Rock for their occasional retirement from the world.

For years to come it was in my thought, as in much of my writing, to seek also to bring again in [to] imaginative life the old sacred places—Slievenamon, Knocknarea—all that reverence that hung—above all—about conspicuous hills. But I wished by my writings and those of the school I hoped to found to have a secret symbolical relation to these mysteries, for in that way, I thought, there will be a greater richness, a greater claim upon the love of the soul, doctrine without exhortation and rhetoric.[17]

Yeats also observed at one time that "civilization is a magnificent illusion which conceals from our eyes the agony of life."[18] This statement indicates quite clearly that Yeats is not escaping from reality but to reality, the same view of reality that he saw in Katherine Tynan's third book of poetry:

> . . . in thus gaining nationality of style, Miss Tynan has found herself and found the world around her. The landscapes are no more taken from the tapestry-like scenery of Rossetti and his imitators, but from the grey Dublin hills.[19]

Sligo and the West of Ireland did for Yeats what Clondalkin and Dublin did for Katherine Tynan.

Directly connected with Yeats's use of specific landscapes are his references to the animals and plants that inhabit these areas. Yeats's poems are very heavily populated with various forms of animal and vegetable life, and in such a natural way that the reader is not so much aware of their importance as he is conscious of their presence, just as the average person is aware of the natural life around him without thinking about it. With a few obvious exceptions such as the rose, animal and plant life —mice, worms, marigolds, and the like—are presented on a level that is almost subconscious. We know they are there, but their presence is so natural in context that we think no more of it. Yet their existence is very important to the total meaning of the poems.

Concerning the poetry written before 1889, Forrest Reid observes that "on nearly every page we meet with the wild, delightful creatures Mr. Yeats himself met with in the rambles of his boyhood."[20] The rose did not overpower all the lesser flowers and animals in Yeats's poetry. Small birds, animals, and flowers appear just as frequently in the poems published between 1889 and 1900, and Yeats realizes the importance of their function. In the first poem in *The Rose,* "To the Rose upon the Rood of Time," the Rose is seen as the power that relates the poet to the world of "common things that crave" (l. 15). The worm and the field-mouse are integral parts of the world of "heavy mortal hopes" (l. 18), a world Yeats knows he must not lose while seeking the "strange things said / By God to the bright hearts of those long dead" (ll. 19–20). For valid poetry, the two worlds must mesh and mingle; they must be seen as one universe.

Yeats was aware of the importance of the function of animal and plant life throughout his career as a poet. From the very first, he senses the coexistence of the two worlds, and he illustrates their coterminous existence through animal and plant imagery of the same sort found in the Irish poetry. Even though his earliest poetry may seem artificial to the modern ear, Yeats counters the artificiality of Arcadia with a constant undertone of living reality. In *The Island of Statues* alone, the following plants and animals are mentioned at least once, and in some cases many times: daffodil, lilac, pansy, ash, willow, cypress, pine, alder, foxglove, rose, lily, sloe berries, hawthorn; heron, sheep, squirrel, crane, panther, owl, drake, woodpecker, grasshopper, bee, adder, moth, wolf, boar, steer, cuckoo, robin, lynx, kine, mouse, cankerworm, fish, kestrel, frog, otter. In addition, there are many general references to trees, flowers, and animals. The little pastoral play literally teems with life.

The poems on Indian subjects, which through mood, tone, and subject matter are the most languorous of Yeats's early poetry, do not, as one might expect, have as many references to plants and animals as Yeats's other poems. Lesser life is nevertheless present, often a more exotic life, such as the peahens and parrot in "The Indian to His Love," but sometimes a life just as common to Ireland as to India. "Anashuya and Vijaya" contains the following: corn, flocks, panthers, poppies, flamingoes, the lion, birds, deer, antelope, the hound, lambs, kine, flies, mice.

In the Irish poetry, as Mr. Reid suggests, the animals and plants are more specifically Irish, and they do occur on virtually every page. With the exception of the rose and the lily, which more often, as in *The Shadowy Waters* and in the poems about the rose, have specifically Pre-Raphaelite and Rosicrucian overtones, the lesser life not only suggests motion; it also affirms the presence of life itself and testifies to the continuing existence of the mundane world in the presence of myth, legend, and fantasy. Taken together with the rose and the lily, the life of earth forms a background tapestry for the whole of the poetry, providing the reader with continuous reminders that the world he knows has not been abandoned or rejected.

Significantly, in "The Man Who Dreamed of Faeryland" the world of nature provides the visions of the land of faerie. The man standing in Dromahair and, later, by the well of Scanavin is told of the other world by extremely commonplace creatures and objects—a pile of fish, a lugworm, a small knot-grass. The fish

> . . . sang what gold morning or evening sheds
> Upon a woven world-forgotten isle
> Wheie a people love beside the ravelled seas;
> That Time can never mar a lover's vows
> Under that woven changeless roof of boughs.
>   (ll. 7–11)

The lugworm

> Sang that somewhere to north or west or south
> There dwelt a gay, exulting, gentle race
> Under the golden or the silver skies.
>   (ll. 19–21)

The knot-grass

> Sang where—unnecessary cruel voice—
> Old silence bids its chosen race rejoice.
>   (ll. 30–31)[21]

In this poem the man is disturbed: at the end he "has found no comfort in the grave," but the world of faerie and the world of nature are seen to be directly interrelated.

By their functions as a motif of reality, as a background for the major concern, and—sometimes—as a link between man and the supernatural, the animals and plants serve to augment and amplify Yeats's use of the landscape. In all of Yeats's early poetry—on Arcadian, Indian, or Irish subjects—they reinforce the value of the natural world. The animals and plants, especially in the Arcadian and Indian poetry, provide the reader with a link of familiarity and make the setting seem less removed and foreign. In the specifically Irish poetry, these functions become more effective because the plants and animals are more tightly integrated in the totality of the poem. The landscape is already real; the animals and plants add to the existing reality. Their primary effect here is to link the legendary world to the present. We are in a world far from cities, and sometimes in a misty world of legend, but Yeats always indicates that we are in an eternal world that is always present. In "The Madness of King Goll," for example, Yeats immediately plunges us into the times and places of Ireland's legendary past:

> I sat on cushioned otter-skin:
> My word was law from Ith to Emain,
> And shook at Inver Amergin
> The hearts of the world-troubling seamen.
>
> (ll. 1–4)

However, instead of drifting completely into the mists of the past (as he is sometimes accused of doing),[22] through his use of forest life Yeats relates the world of Ith and Emain to the world that is always present:

> And now I wander in the woods
> When summer gluts the golden bees,
> Or in autumnal solitudes
> Arise the leopard-coloured trees;
> Or when along the wintry strands
> The cormorants shiver on their rocks.
>
> (ll. 37–42)

The exotic connotations of "leopard-coloured" are carefully balanced with the "ordinary" creatures, the bees and cormorants, and the four seasons of the Irish climate. Amid the natural seasons, King Goll wanders in the company of the wolf, the deer, and the hares of the forest.

Yeats often suggests motion through the use of small creatures. Animals in Yeats are not used for the sake of imagery alone. In most cases they, like the wind and the leaves in "The Hosting of the Sidhe," are present in the poem because they are present in life, or occasionally, like the hound with one red ear in *The Wanderings of Oisin,* because they are present in Yeats's original source. In specific relation to the poetic dream, the function of the many fish, mice, birds, and the like, is to suggest the constant movement of these lower forms of life:

> Autumn is over the long leaves that love us,
> And over the mice in the barley sheaves;
> Yellow the leaves of the rowan above us,
> And yellow the wet wild-strawberry leaves.
> ("The Falling of the Leaves," ll. 1–4)

Amidst the yellowing decay and coming of the death of winter, Yeats does not overlook the presence of the mice.

The totality of the landscape, then, becomes more than a setting: it is a philosophical entity that, together with the other elements of Yeats's poetic vision, makes the poetry not an abstract criticism of life but the embodiment of life itself. This is not to say that Yeats subscribes to a form of pantheism, nor that he finds in nature the same type of power or inspiration that Wordsworth feels. In Yeats's poetry, the natural surroundings do more than surround: they become an integral part of existence. Man is not detached, and there is no man-nature conflict. Although Yeats does not idealize in the manner of Rousseau, he does consider man and nature to be inseparable. He does not present to us an Eden, and his views of man and environment appear primitivistic only to the modern town- or city-dweller who has lost his intimate relationship with the natural world.

The grounding of the dream in the landscape and, significantly, the location of the retreat on specific islands give a focus that prevents the dream from becoming a mere escape. Nevertheless, there is more evidence in the poetry than the use of Irish places. Professor Rajan cites many passages from *The Shadowy Waters* that indicate that "the reality beyond the world" is really "the world's quintessence";[23] he bolsters his argument that "the higher reality is continuous with the lower" with the imagery in Dectora's climactic speech:

> O flower of the branch, O bird among the leaves,
> O silver fish that my two hands have taken
> Out of the running stream, O morning star,

Trembling in the blue heavens like a white fawn
Upon the misty border of the wood,
Bend lower, that I may cover you with my hair,
For we will gaze upon this world no longer.

(ll. 608-614)

Professor Rajan quotes these lines as "an affirmation of life in
the very act of severance from life,"[24] and he emphasizes the
"progression in the imagery" from flower to morning star and
fawn, from natural life to rebirth and the innocence of the
newly born. He adds, however, that such subtleties in the play
are often misunderstood "because the poetry is at variance with
the dramatic structure, and because both are only fitful embodi-
ments of conceptions which remain evasively defined."[25] The
play should not be condemned, however, because of the evasively
defined conceptions. Even though Yeats's poetry did take a
different direction after the revision of *The Shadowy Waters*
and *The Wind among the Reeds,* we do not have to follow most
of the critics (and Yeats himself) and move joyously along into
the more "mature" and "adult" poetry after a few fleet and
perhaps grudging acknowledgments of the promise shown in
the earlier.[26] The evasive definition, the Celtic Twilight of
the earlier poetry, which seem to cause so many critics, such as
Morton Seiden and Virginia Moore, to stumble, are really neces-
sary and integral parts of the early vision of the dream in which
the truth is perceived. After all, how can the poet be a seeker
when what he is seeking has been found? And what would we
have in the early poetry without the movement of the search?
We would truly have a languid Pre-Raphaelitism, or perhaps
merely a number of charming but relatively inconsequential
poems. Concerning the value of the early poems, in *Yeats's
Iconography* Professor F. A. C. Wilson observes that they are
"at least potentially adult" or a "direct consequence" of Yeats's
knowledge of myth. Professor Wilson affirms the soundness of
Yeats's background in comparative symbolism and "esoteric
archetypes" and states that "even his early poetry has an intellec-
tual substructure as well as a surface richness."[27] Even more than
the "esoteric archetypes," we have along with the myth, in all
the poetry described as "dreamy," a sense of motion, of vitality

such as that Rajan describes in *The Shadowy Waters,* or, to use
currently popular critical terminology, a tension that gives an
inner life to the poetry and awakens a deeper response in the
reader.

Yeats's dream is not of perfect tranquillity, nor is it just a
state in which symbols appear in order to evoke response and
connective emotions. It is a total state, involving movement,
time, a concern with change. The sensation of movement is
evoked in many ways. Often movement is pictured graphically,
as in the lines quoted above from "The Hosting of the Sidhe." In
this poem the reader is borne away in a sense of rushing, sweep-
ing motion. The fast-paced rhythm and the very description of
action in the first four lines immediately draw the reader in as
a participant. The swift rushing is maintained throughout the
poem. At the end, the reader is left with the feeling that he has
been briefly involved in violent motion that has now left him
behind:

> The host is rushing 'twixt night and day,
> And where is there hope or deed as fair?
> Caoilte tossing his burning hair,
> And Niamh calling *Away, come away.*
> (ll. 13-16)

The emotional response of the reader is heightened in this
poem by the use of another method of conveying the feeling of
motion, the evocation of a sense of inner vitality through the
description of smaller, more individual movements:

> *The winds awaken, the leaves whirl round,*
> *Our cheeks are pale, our hair is unbound,*
> *Our breasts are heaving, our eyes are agleam,*
> *Our arms are waving, our lips are apart. . . .*
> (ll. 6-9)

In these lines the Sidhe surge with life, and movement permeates
their whole being. The "smaller" movements of the heaving
breasts, waving arms, whirling leaves are contained within the
"large" movement of the host of the Sidhe riding from Knock-
narea.

In the structure of the poems related to the theme of poet-seeker, such as *The Wanderings of Oisin,* there can be discerned three levels directly informed by motion or lack of motion. *Oisin* is dominated and controlled by Oisin's wanderings, his search: in this sense it is all motion. Yet in another sense the poem is all stillness. Time is suspended for Oisin. His travels last for three hundred years; he remains on each island for one hundred years; when he again sets foot physically upon Ireland, he ages immediately. He is young throughout his travels; when he talks of them in his dialogue with Saint Patrick, he is "bent, and bald, and blind" (l. 1). Within the stillness of the time suspension there is the movement of lesser life—the birds, the deer, the hounds. Herein lies the tension of motion and rest. In this poem there are worlds within worlds, from the macrocosmic to the microcosmic.

The complexity of time, motion, stillness, and dream, of sound and silence, gradually becomes intensified as the poem progresses. First, in Oisin's travels outward from Ireland to the first island, and onward to the second and third islands, time becomes confused. Each time Oisin leaves the shore for the open sea, his sense of time becomes blurred; each time, until he leaves the last island and Remembrance returns to him, the same is repeated with only slight modifications:

> I know not if days passed or hours . . .
> (I, 133)

> I do not know if days
> Or hours passed by . . .
> (II, 19-20)

> Were we days long or hours long in riding . . . ?
> (III, 9)

Accompanied by sound, or, on the last segment of the journey, the consciousness of lack of sound, Oisin travels farther away from the world he knows into the world of eternal mists and disillusion. In the first part of the journey, leaving Ireland, Niamh sings continuous songs of the other world; between the first island and the second, her song is "troubled" by tears; after leaving the second island, Niamh no longer sings.

Paralleling the intensifying sorrow of Niamh, the islands are progressively more removed from active, physical life and more and more involved with life as seen in a dream. In the first island, called significantly "The Island of the Living" in the 1889 version, there are many contrasts between action and stillness. After the mysterious journey over the water, we are introduced to the world of twilight and the dream. However, even though we see Aengus in his hall dreaming "a Druid dream of the end of days" (I, 219), when even "the stars are to wane" and a literal twilight exists throughout, there is the contrasting action of the Immortals, the movement of the dance, the sounds of the harp and the song. In eternal summer, Oisin engages in the traditional heroic sports of hunting, fishing, and wrestling. As we leave the Island of the Living, Yeats shows us a vignette of action and inaction that, in essence, summarizes the existence of the first island. In the golden light of evening, some of the Immortals move among the fountains, dance, and wander hand in hand; others sit in dreams on the water's edge, singing and gazing at the setting sun while the birds keep time to the music.

On the second island, called "The Island of Victories" in the 1889 version, Oisin finds himself in an atmosphere of greater mystery. On The Island of Fears, as it was named in the definitive edition, eternity consists of actions perpetually repeated. In the attempt to deliver a maiden chained to two ancient eagles, Oisin fights with a demon. This action begins an endless fight, for the demon perpetually renews himself: Oisin fights and defeats the demon; after the third day of the victory feast, the demon reappears. Thus, for one hundred years Oisin endures, without dreams, fears, languor, or fatigue, "an endless feast. / An endless war" (II, 223–224).

When Oisin reaches the third island, the Island of the Sleepers ("The Island of Forgetfulness" in the 1889 version), Yeats's subtlety in dealing with rest and motion reaches its height. Oisin lives only in dreaming of life:

> So lived I and lived not, so wrought I and wrought not,
>   with creatures of dreams,

> In a long iron sleep, as a fish in the water goes dumb
>   as a stone.
>
>   (III, 95-96)

In describing the island, Yeats tells us that "no live creatures
lived there" (III, 19). In context, however, much life is suggested
in the description of deathly stillness:

> But the trees grew taller and closer, immense in
>   their wrinkling bark;
> Dropping; a murmurous dropping; old silence and
>   that one sound;
> For no live creatures lived there, no weasels moved
>   in the dark:
> Long sighs arose in our spirits, beneath us bubbled
>   the ground.
>
>   (III, 17-20)

The trees seem to loom larger in Oisin's eyes; the trees and the
ground exude noises; Oisin thinks of weasels. A few lines later
the horse whinnies when he catches sight of the huge, white,
sleeping bodies. The presence of owls (in spite of the statement
made in line 19) provides an effective contrast of life with the
slumberers:

> So long were they sleeping, the owls had builded
>   their nests in their locks,
> Filling the fibrous dimness with long generations
>   of eyes.
> And over the limbs and the valley the slow owls
>   wandered and came,
> Now in a place of star-fire, and now in a shadow-
>   place wide;
> And the chief of the huge white creatures, his knees
>   in the soft star-flame,
> Lay loose in a place of shadow: we drew the reins by
>   his side.
>
>   (III, 39-44)

In these lines Yeats gives us not only life but continuing life, with
"generations" of owls. Perception is suggested by the use of "eyes"

in line 40. The busy and ordinary activity of nest-building complements the action of Niamh and Oisin in reining their horses, while the slow wandering movement, related through inversion in line 41, effectively complements the mysterious sleepers. In addition, the movement of life is sustained in the mind of the reader throughout this island of sleep-enchantment by frequent references to life in the world of man as Oisin relates to Saint Patrick the things the island caused him to forget: "How the falconer follows the falcon in the weeds of the heron's plot" (III, 79); "How the slow, blue-eyed oxen of Finn low sadly at evening tide" (III, 84). Yeats thus maintains an awareness of life and motion even when describing their absence. No matter how removed the dream world is from the world of men—and the islands visited by Oisin are fabled and eternal, removed from time —the dream never loses consciousness of reality. Even in the early Arcadian play *The Island of Statues,* in which one might expect from the very nature of the Arcadian subject matter a complete removal from the world, the sleepers awake from their enchantment asking about men and events from the lives they were living before the spell was cast upon them.

A clear example of Yeats's use of various types of motion and motion suggestion, of time and timelessness within the dream, can be seen in the short, nine-line "Love Song from the Gaelic," which appeared in *Poems and Ballads of Young Ireland* (1888):

> My love, we will go, we will go, I and you,
> And away in the woods we will scatter the dew;
> And the salmon behold, and the ousel too,
> My love, we will hear, I and you, we will hear,
> The calling afar of the doe and the deer.
> And the bird in the branches will cry for us clear,
> And the cuckoo unseen in his festival mood;
> And death, oh my fair one, will never come near
> In the bosom afar of the fragrant wood.

This very early and immature lyric is quoted here for an important reason. Many critics, and Yeats himself, would probably refer to it as "escape poetry"; yet, even in this admittedly trivial lyric (it was never published in any edition of Yeats's works), it is clear that the so-called "escape" is not a true flight from reality, and that this escape is part of the seeker theme and an important part of the complex poetic dream. In this small poem Yeats introduces the important elements found in later, more sophisticated poetry dealing with the seeker. As in "The Stolen Child," "The Hosting of the Sidhe," and *The Wanderings of Oisin,* there is the summons to go. The world into which the loved one is summoned is eternal and timeless: "death . . . will never come near"; but it is also a forest world filled with creatures. This poem does represent a yearning for the pastoral, but it is a pastoral that exists among familiar and living things. When the eternal world is gained, the best of the transitory world is not lost.

In discussing Yeats's poetry, one must be cautious in making a distinction between eternal and transitory states of existence. The question of time in Yeats's poetic dream needs further investigation, for here we reach an ambiguity that is unresolved. It is too easy to conclude that in the later verse Byzantium provides the solution when the poet is "gather[ed]" into "the artifice of eternity," for even in "Sailing to Byzantium" Yeats echoes the concern for old age that pervades his later verse and that is actually a manifestation of a concern found in Yeats from the beginning: Can man, through his art, conquer time? Though man dies and buildings fall into ruins, Yeats hopes that poetry is eternal. But it is a hope, not a certainty:

> I, the poet William Yeats,
> With old mill boards and sea-green slates,
> And smithy work from the Gort forge,
> Restored this tower for my wife George;
> And may these characters remain
> When all is ruin once again.
> ("To be Carved on a Stone at Thoor Ballylee")

As Yeats prophetically predicts, this very old tower—Yeats liked to think it was Norman, though no one seems to know its age— did fall into ruin (it is now being restored), and these lines, carved on a stone of the tower, do remain. Somehow, though, Yeats's hope seems wistful; the inscription of Ozymandias is the best one can hope for.

The lines carved on the tower comprise the statement of a practical man and the enunciation of a conclusion that is pessimistic and almost cynical for a poet so conscious of the importance of his art. Yeats obviously did not operate from the philosophy implied by these lines throughout his poetic career. In his use of the dream it is clear that he was searching for the true relationship existing between time and his art.

The dream state, by its very nature, involves a focus on time different from that of the waking state, and under special conditions the dream state can involve a negation of time. The true vision pierces eternity, and a state of enchantment, such as that of Oisin or the sleepers in *The Island of Statues,* can suspend time. If immortal creatures could be found, it should be in the supernatural world, but for Yeats there seems to be some doubt:

> A man has a hope for heaven,
> But soulless a fairy dies.

Is there, then, a world of eternity? If so, where does it exist?

In the poetic dream, one does not escape from reality: one escapes to reality. The true meaning of escape—the meaning indicated earlier—and the true Celtic Twilight can be seen in the short poem "Into the Twilight." The spiritual condition of the poet and the summons to the quest are contained in the first two lines:

> Out-worn heart, in a time out-worn,
> Come clear of the nets of wrong and right.

To find reality, the poet must escape the petty, middle-class world of the dull, smugly complacent, and spiritually ignorant shopkeeper, the "nets of wrong and right" that can ensnare a person into a world in which everything is seen in terms of black and white, good and evil; the same world discussed later in connection with Saint Patrick in *The Wanderings of Oisin.* If one can leave modern city life, the poem implies, "Eire is always young" (1. 5), and in Ireland the poet can find reality:

Come, heart, where hill is heaped upon hill:
For there the mystical brotherhood
Of sun and moon and hollow and wood
And willow and stream work out their will.

(ll. 9–12)

Eternity and the dream are found in the soil and in nature. The poet is summoned to leave the "nets of wrong and right," but he does not enter a clear, uncomplicated paradise. Yeats juxtaposes the "grey twilight" with the "dew of the morn"; the heart is summoned to laughter and sighs; the heart laughs in the greyness and sighs in the shining dew (ll. 3–4). The loneliness of God coexists with the "mystical brotherhood" of nature. This is the eternal youth of Ireland, which will remain even though "hope fall from you and love decay."

"Time and the world are ever in flight." Yeats is affirming these things that endure, the "shining dew" and the "grey twilight." Hope and love do not endure, for they are the kind of hope and love that can be destroyed "in fires of a slanderous tongue." In this context, Yeats could be implying a Neoplatonic distinction between higher and lower types of love and hope. The modern world, the world of the slanderous tongue, the world containing the type of love and hope prone to decay, is most probably the world he writes about later, in which "Romantic Ireland" has been replaced by men who

. . . fumble in a greasy till
And add the halfpence to the pence
And prayer to shivering prayer, until
You have dried the marrow from the bone.

("September, 1913")

In his radio talk "Players and Painted Stage," which has been reprinted by Denis Donoghue in *The Integrity of Yeats,* Frank Kermode quotes Yeats's observation that art is "the struggle of the dream with the world." Kermode defines the dream as "a transcendent reality, the truth of the imagination." According to Kermode, the world is more complex than the mere opposite of the dream; it is not simply a place to be hated and shunned.

He accurately defines the world as it is seen in Yeats's poetry:

The world is something to be both hated and loved: the spiritless sphere of realists, shopkeepers, "thinkers," and also the place of admired animal vitality—"the young in one another's arms"—and heroic action.[28]

The poet is summoned not from the world but from *a* world, the world of pettiness and minor values, the "nets of wrong and right," in which the major values are obscured and lost. Yeats states his position quite clearly in "To Ireland in the Coming Times," which was entitled more explicitly in the first printing in 1892 as "Apologia Addressed to Ireland in the Coming Days." This poem is the personal credo of Yeats as an Irish poet, and even though couched in the language and style of the early poetry, it is a credo he never abandoned. In the first four lines, Yeats fits himself into a tradition and shows that he is escaping *into* a world of artistic purpose:

> Know, that I would accounted be
> True brother of a company
> That sang, to sweeten Ireland's wrong,
> Ballad and story, rann and song.

In the world of the Irish poetic tradition, time operates in a special way in relation to art:

> When Time began to rant and rage
> The measure of her flying feet
> Made Ireland's heart begin to beat;
> And Time bade all his candles flare
> To light a measure here and there;
> And may the thoughts of Ireland brood
> Upon a measured quietude.
> (ll. 10-16)

Perhaps Time's candles can, for a moment, "light a measure" even for the world of the "greasy till."

When living in a world necessarily and unavoidably governed by time, the poet is in a state of existence in which the dream is essential:

> Because, to him who ponders well,
> My rhymes more than their rhyming tell
> Of things discovered in the deep,
> Where only body's laid asleep.
>
>   (ll. 19–22)

This is one of Yeats's clearest statements of the function of the
dream in poetry. The dreams supply the meaning of the poetry,
and they become the key to the unity for which the poet is
searching.

An examination of Yeats's revisions of this poem will con-
firm the continued and steady importance of the dream through-
out his career; the revisions also reveal an earlier emphasis on the
dream. The version quoted here is that of the definitive edition.
Although Yeats made no revisions that directly change the
meaning of this poem, he was more explicit in the versions that
appeared in and before the 1924 revision of *Poems* (1895). In
this and earlier editions, lines 21 and 22 read: "Of the dim wis-
doms old and deep, / That God gives unto man in sleep." In all
versions of this poem, both early and late, Yeats alludes, in the
lines immediately following, to mysterious forces that come
"about [his] table" through the dream. These forces are called
"magical powers" in 1892, "elemental beings" in all versions
from 1895 through 1924, and "elemental creatures" in the
definitive edition. Yeats was always aware that dreams provide
the poetic insight.

In "To Ireland in the Coming Times," Yeats reveals that he is
living in an intermediary state between the materialistic world of
pounds, shillings, and pence and the eternal world for which he
is searching. The dream is an essential part of the poetic search,
and that search is not over: unity has not been attained and knowl-
edge is not complete; therefore, the ambiguities, the "vagueness"
and cloudiness often deplored in Yeats's early poetry are un-
avoidable, and indeed essential, at this stage of artistic develop-
ment.[29] The last stanza of this poem gives us the perspective
we need in order to understand the dream and its importance
to the poetic search:

> I cast my heart into my rhymes,
> That you, in the dim coming times,
> May know how my heart went with them
> After the red-rose-bordered hem.
> (ll. 45-48)

In these lines the dream and the poetry itself are very closely connected. In the short life allotted to man, the poet's heart went "after the red-rose-bordered hem" that is specifically Ireland, the hem of Cathleen ni Houlihan; but by suggestion, Yeats is following all that is implied by the red rose. In his note to "Aedh Hears the Cry of the Sedge," Yeats observes that "the Rose has been for many centuries a symbol of spiritual love and supreme beauty." He goes on to enumerate many uses of the rose in religion and in poetry. In the notes to *The Rose,* Yeats says that "the quality symbolised as The Rose differs from the Intellectual Beauty of Shelley and of Spenser in that I have imagined it as suffering with man and not as something pursued and seen from afar." This last note was written in 1925, and Yeats tells us that he noticed this quality of the rose "upon reading these poems for the first time for several years." The element of pursuit is implied, however, by the use of the word *after* in the last line. Nevertheless, the retrospective statement in the note does give an added insight. A concept such as intellectual beauty is a logical goal for the poetic search, and Yeats's use of the rose in many of his early poems makes it clear that the rose is one symbol of the goal of his search. Here, though, we see the goal as something attainable, even as something present. The rose can be seen in the poetic dream.

The dreaminess, cloudiness, and ambiguity found in Yeats are usually defended or condemned primarily on artistic and philosophical grounds, following one or more of the standard methods of literary criticism. What many critics fail to see, or at least fail to mention, is the strong element of plain common sense found in Yeats. Like the peasants he admired, he could combine the affairs of daily life with glimpses and concern for the supernatural. If the trait of common sense is overlooked, there

are unsurmountable difficulties in interpreting Yeats's poetry
and prose. (On the other hand, it should be noted that Yeats is
not a literate Margery Kempe, who was so bound to life on
earth that her relation with Christ, as seen in her *Booke,* is simply
another sexual affair.) Such critics as Harold Bloom, for example,
have difficulties with Yeats's religion and his mysticism.[30] The
confusion found in Yeats's poetry and in his comments about
his symbols and his philosophy is understandable, and even
sometimes erased, when they are read in the light of such state-
ments as those found in the lines "To be Carved on a Stone at
Thoor Ballylee," which are quoted above. Yeats accepts the fact
that man and his creations are not eternal; at the same time, ideas
and thoughts can remain.

Yeats's often-mentioned concern with sex also recognizes the
transitory nature of human existence along with the concepts of
repetition and continuity. A sexual moment, such as the union
of Zeus and Leda, is fleeting. It lasts, like all sexual encounters,
only a brief moment; yet it is also an act of the renewal of life,
unique in itself while being similar to other sexual acts through-
out the generations of man. As readers of his later poetry are
very much aware, Yeats was quite concerned with being an old
man—even a "dirty old man." The life of one man will end, but
the concern with the continuity of Life is ever present.

There are two methods, however, by which man can achieve
permanence. One, the most discussed in relation to Yeats, is to
see things and events as parts of a total Unity: Zeus's encounter
with Leda, which ushered in one age, will be repeated again and
again with each new age and, in a less important form, within
each age. Thus, as Helen of Troy lives in Maud Gonne, the act
is symbolically permanent through eternal repetition. The other
method is a practical one: the attempt of man to preserve ideas,
objects, and himself for as long as possible. Snickers usually come
forth when someone mentions the Steinach operation for re-
juvenation that a London surgeon performed on Yeats in 1934.
However, even though the operation was mentioned to Yeats in
jest,[31] Yeats underwent the surgery with enthusiasm and serious-
ness. Yeats may seem foolish, but this is an attempt by the man
to restore himself and preserve himself and his art for a longer
time.

> Could Crazy Jane put off old age
> And ranting time renew,
> Could that old god rise up again
> We'd drink a can or two,
> And out and lay our leadership
> On country and on town,
> Throw likely couples into bed
> And knock the others down.
> ("Three Songs to the One Burden," ll. 19-26)

Yeats said in *The Death of Synge* (1928) that "Ireland is ruined by abstractions."[32] Even though this statement was published only eleven years before the poet's death, it is not the thought of the "later Yeats" as opposed to the "earlier." In one form or another, this concept was always a part of Yeats's poetic theory. The oral tradition mentioned elsewhere in this study emphasizes that poetry is both human and eternal. It is produced by the voice of a man and is handed down from man to man. It is of the moment, and it is also eternal in its continuity and in the making of poetry.

In "To Ireland in the Coming Times," especially in the last four lines quoted above, the poems are the proof of the poetic search. The "rhymes more than their rhyming tell" (l. 20), but the meaning does not exist alone. The rhyming itself is part of the poetic dream. Yeats's own ideas on the speaking of verse indicate the true function of poetic technique. In reference to two lyrics from *The Countess Cathleen* printed in the first issue of *Beltaine* (May 1899), Yeats observes that the lyrics

are not sung, but spoken, or rather chanted, to music, as the old poems were probably chanted by bards and rhapsodists. Even when the words of a song, sung in the ordinary way, are heard at all, their own proper rhythm and emphasis are lost, or partly lost, in the rhythm and emphasis of the music. A lyric which is spoken or chanted to music should, on the other hand, reveal its meaning, and its rhythm so become indissoluble in the memory.[33]

In this particular method of uniting the sound and the sense, Yeats was trying to return as far as possible to the spirit and technique of the ancient bards. T. W. Rolleston informs us in

Myths and Legends of the Celtic Race that "the *fili,* or professional poets . . . were a branch of the Druidic order," and the Druids constituted "a sacerdotal organization, which administered the whole system of religious and secular learning and literature."[34] Yeats did not, of course, see himself as a priest-magician, but he could envision a revival of lost but spiritually necessary arts, in which the speaking of poetry would become an invocation or a reenactment of the dream.

CHAPTER TWO

THE ENVIRONMENT OF THE QUEST:

THE PHYSICAL AND
THE SPIRITUAL

The dream opens for us the world of the poetic quest and the
figure of the poet-seeker. Yeats, like Keats in "Ode to a Night-
ingale," does not completely understand the dream; yet he does
know that somewhere within the dream there is wisdom. In a
sketch entitled "The Golden Age" from *The Celtic Twilight,* he
recounts one occasion when he "saw with blinding distinctness,
as I lay between sleeping and waking . . ."; and in *The Bookman,*
December 1893, he published these lines:

> Wisdom and dreams are one,
> For dreams are the flowers ablow,
> And Wisdom the fruit of the garden:
> God planted him long ago.[35]

The dream is the environment of the search: and the dream
alone can direct the seeker toward his goal. The Celtic Twilight
can be seen as the twilight of the dream, and the dreamlike
atmosphere of many of the early poems, the mists through which
Forgael and Oisin travel, are the hazy atmosphere of the dream
that leads to wisdom, the environment of the poetic search.

The universe of the seeker includes the natural and the super-
natural, the past, the present, and perhaps the future. As in a
dream, these various elements become fused, intermingled, and
juxtaposed in the poetry. Forgael, in the 1906 version of *The*

Shadowy Waters, has hope for wisdom when he says to Dectora:

> . . . we grow immortal
> . . . .
> . . . and dreams,
> That have had dreams for father, live in us.
> (ll. 616–619)

Forgael is in a world of mists and mystery: he is crossing un-
charted seas to the world's end. He is confident and determined
in his search, yet the destination is never clear. The reader is
always uncertain as to what lies at the end of the world. Forgael's
search, thus, becomes both purposeful and shadowy. In this
sense, Forgael is typical of all of Yeats's early seekers, such as
the Old Knight, Oisin, and Fergus. All are confident that the
search is of primary importance—perhaps that it is the only
thing of importance. The route traveled, however, is uncharted
and leads to the unknown.

The vagueness and mystery are essential to the world of the
poet-seeker as he is seen in the early poetry. Yeats was himself
a poet-seeker; his poetry is written not from the perspective of
the mature artist—or perhaps the medieval artist—who views his
universe as a whole, but from the point of view of the artist who
is still seeking for a unity of vision that his faith tells him must
exist somewhere.

Although the mists of the Celtic Twilight are necessary in the
early poetry, for all is not known with certainty, there is a con-
sistent pattern of thought throughout this body of poetry that
indicates that the poet has some grounds for his confidence.
Yeats tells us repeatedly in his prose writings that unity of vision
and being did exist at times during the past until the Renaissance
came along to shatter it.[36] Since that time man's view of life
and the universe has been fragmentary. Yeats, however, was not
trying to recapture the past, though the past should never go
ignored. He wanted to recapture the visionary experience of the
universe and life as unity, to find a vision in which there is no
attempt to juggle two worlds or to reject one world for another.
This, then, is the poetic search: the search for totality of poetic
vision, a search that is not impossible (others have succeeded),

but a search that is very difficult in the modern world.

If the reader is conscious of the pastoral framework as it is adapted by Yeats's individual concern, it becomes quite clear that we are not dealing with "escape poetry." The "place apart" mentioned earlier is the Celtic Twilight, the universe of the poet-seeker. The world of the search is not the conventional world, and Yeats's attempt to transcend traditional patterns of thought should not be seen as an escape from the world of "reality." Yeats's escape is not a flight; it is an essential beginning of the poetic quest.

Alex Zwerdling, in his excellent essay "W. B. Yeats: Variations on the Visionary Quest," states that Yeats refused to accept one world, either the perfect or the imperfect, at the expense of the other, and this refusal "inspired his attempt to reconcile the two apparently opposing realms."[37] Zwerdling goes on to say that many critics have misunderstood "this restless search for an escape from the implications of an antinomic religious belief."[38] Although he does not carry his argument to its logical conclusion, he comes close enough to see that Yeats was attracted to "the idea of an actual world intersected at numerous points by a spiritual one."[39] However, Zwerdling states that Yeats does not use this idea until the last fifteen or twenty years of his career.[40] He does not see that the early poetry, as well as the later, attempts to show or find a basic unity. The escape in Yeats, even in the early Yeats, is not an escape from the world but an escape from the idea commonly accepted in Western thought that there are two worlds, and that one is compelled to belong to one or the other.

Following Yeats's own comments in a letter to Katherine Tynan (14 March 1888), critics have seized upon "The Stolen Child" as an example of Yeats's early poetry of escape from the real world. In his letter to Miss Tynan, Yeats says:

I have much improved "Mosada" by polishing the verse here and there. I have noticed some things about my poetry I did not know before, in this process of correction; for instance, that it is almost all a flight into fairy-land from the real world, and a summons to that flight. The chorus to "The Stolen Child" sums it up—that it is not the poetry of insight and knowledge, but of longing and complaint—the cry of the heart against necessity. I hope some day to alter that and (to) write poetry of insight and knowledge.[41]

No book on Yeats seems complete without quotation of or reference to this passage. However valuable a poet's own statements may be, we should not take one comment as a complete critical dictum. For one thing, this passage comments on only one aspect of the poetry, and one part of the particular poem. The chorus to "The Stolen Child" does express a summons of escape:

> Come away, O human child!
> To the waters and the wild
> With a faery, hand in hand,
> For the world's more full of weeping
> than you can understand.

However, the chorus is not the whole poem. In the first three stanzas the world of faerie has definite and specific relations with the world of man. In the first stanza, the "leafy island" is located off the rocky "highland / Of Sleuth Wood," and the same island is populated with herons and water-rats. Thus the hiding place of the fairies has a specific geographical location—it is a real island in County Sligo—and it is populated by ordinary creatures familiar to the world of man. In the second stanza, the fairy dances take place at "furthest Rosses," another specific location in County Sligo. In the third stanza, the fairies enchant trout in the pools and fern-banked streams above Glen-Car. By suggesting concrete reality through the use of small, ordinary creatures of the countryside and proper names belonging to real places, Yeats makes it quite evident that the world of faerie and the world of man, at least at these points, are closely intermingled.

In this particular poem, also, the world of faerie and the world of man have a very important element in common: a certain uneasiness, with an underlying hint of evil. There is no Eden here. In addition to the Weltschmerz expressed in the line "For the world's more full of weeping than you can understand," the human world is seen to be "full of troubles" and "anxious in its sleep" (ll. 22–23). The unhappiness and implied guilt in the anxious sleep of the human world is matched in the other world by the actions of the fairies, who enchant the trout with "unquiet dreams" (l. 34). In the earliest editions of this poem (*The Irish Monthly*, December 1886, and *The Wanderings of Oisin and*

Other Poems, 1889, 1892), Yeats had "And whispering in their ears / We give them evil dreams." The change from "evil" to "unquiet" in the later versions of the poem makes the suggestion less specific, but there is no real change in the suggestive meaning: The actions of the fairies are malicious. On a small scale, the world of faerie creates unrest in the world of man with the evil or unquiet dreams of the trout and the stolen cherries (1. 8), and on a larger scale with the stolen child himself.

In the final juxtaposition of the two spheres, the child is led away "solemn-eyed" (1. 43). In the context of the last stanza, one is uncertain whether the child is solemn-eyed because of apprehension, because of the loss of the simple, pastoral world he is leaving, because of the world into which he is going, or possibly because he has seen the reality of both worlds.

In this poem, Yeats does not actually contrast the world of faerie with the human world; he mingles the two as he felt they were mingled in the minds of the peasants—and as he wanted them to be mingled in his own mind. This poem is clearly a partial expression of the state of mind involved in Yeats's search. "The Stolen Child" is not an expression of a Pre-Raphaelite escape: within the smooth sounds of the rhythms and the almost languid repetition of the refrain, there is an emotional tension created by the meaning of the words themselves. Tranquillity mingles with sadness and foreboding. Many elements of Yeats's search are here: the island, the aura of enchantment, and above all the apprehensiveness and the fear, found principally in the solemn-eyed child—reminiscent of the preternaturally old children found in some of Hardy's novels. There is a fear in the spiritual, a fear that appears even in Yeats's earliest poetry.

The world of faerie is not a pure world of peace, light, and joy. The presence of evil in the supernatural produces an uneasiness and a tension that add another dimension to the mood of sorrow often found in Yeats's "fairy poems." Yeats's earlier poems may seem languid and soft to the modern ear accustomed to Yeats's later poetry and to the harsher lines of Eliot and his school, but even in the most melodic of Yeats's early fairy poems there is often a tone of desperation and immediacy that removes them from the realm of romantic longing. A good example would be an untitled lyric first published in 1885 and later in that year included in *The Island of Statues,* the first two lines of which were quoted in the previous chapter.

> A man has the fields of heaven,
> But soulless a fairy dies,
> As a leaf that is old, and withered, and cold,
> When the wintry vapours rise.
>
> Soon shall our wings be stilled,
> And our laughter over and done:
> So let us dance where the yellow lance
> Of the barley shoots in the sun.
>
> So let us dance on fringèd waves,
> And shout at the wisest owls
> In their downy caps, and startle the naps
> Of the dreaming water-fowls,
>
> And fight for the black sloe-berries,
> For soulless a fairy dies,
> As a leaf that is old, and withered, and cold,
> When the wintry vapours rise.

A more than casual reading will reveal something deeper than the simplicity of juvenilia. This poem may sound languid and soft, but the gentle tone contains a complexity of internal tension. Within the basic winter-summer contrast there is a carpe diem urgency in the logical since-then structure of stanzas two, three, and four. The languor in the poem is actually the human reaction to the world of faerie, which man believes to be carefree and delightful. In actuality, however, the world of faerie is not eternal but temporary—a brief moment of existence in which the present is affirmed, not because the present is always here but because there is no future. The desperation is revealed not merely in open and repeated statement ("But soulless a fairy dies" and "Soon shall our wings be stilled," but also in the very actions contained in these three stanzas. In contrast to "stilled" in line 5, there are "laughter," "dance," "shoots," "shout," "startle," "fight"—words expressing vigorous and even violent life. The fairy world is frantic, and more temporal than what is usually called "the temporal world." Their activity takes place amid the actions of the world familiar to man. If their actions are removed, we are left with a peaceful, pastoral world, a world of barley in the sun, fringed waves, wise owls, dreaming water fowl, a world that can contemplate the fields of heaven. The urgency of the actions and vitality of the fairies seems to be a direct result of the knowledge that they will soon die eternally.

The elements of fear and apprehension seen in these early poems show the reality of Yeats's vision. These are no "trumpery little English fairies," as Louis MacNeice would have us believe;[42] they are the fairies of the Irish supernatural world, which, as Professor F. A. C. Wilson observes in *Yeats's Iconography*, "combine a fabulous physical pulchritude with a settled malignance."[43] The world of faerie is a world of beauty and evil: an escape to fairyland is not an escape to prelapsarian Eden, but to Eden after the Fall. It is very much the "real" world in that it contains many of the desires, motivations, even the objects, of the mortal world.

It really matters very little whether or not Yeats is contradicting a traditional concept of the world of faerie. The important point is that Yeats is showing the similarity and fusion of the natural and the supernatural, the physical and the spiritual.

Through an examination of the two Byzantium poems, Zwerdling does reach the conclusion that "in Yeats's final view of the visionary . . . physical and spiritual are seen as inseparable, mutually dependent, and simultaneous."[44] According to his study, the earlier "Sailing to Byzantium" presents a "dichotomy between physical and spiritual" that the speaker never reconciles. When the speaker states, "Once out of nature I shall never take / My bodily form from any natural thing," he abandons the one world for the other. On the other hand, in "Byzantium" the two worlds are joined by the trips of the dolphins, and "the mortal world provides the necessary food and fuel to keep the immortal world alive"; Zwerdling also points out that even the process of mortal becoming immortal "is described in metaphors of eating and burning."[45]

A brief examination of the early poetry will reveal the same type of physical, mortal, and earthly metaphors that Zwerdling cites to support his statements about "Byzantium." The creatures of earth do not travel between the two worlds like the dolphins, but, as we have seen, they are very much present in both worlds —and it might be mentioned that Oisin and Niamh travel on horses—magical horses, to be sure, but spiritual equivalents to those on earth. In *The Shadowy Waters,* Forgael has expected to find an immortal love, but he finds that a mortal love must accompany him. He is going to "where the world ends," but part of the world goes with him. At the end of the play, Dectora's hair is gathered about him to hide him from the world. This is a veil image, but a very earthy, sensuous veil. Also, the action of *The Shadowy Waters* takes place after Forgael has left the island where he received the magic harp. The island clearly indicates a separation from the world, but the separation is not absolute. The island is a milestone on the journey and the place where Forgael makes important contact with the spiritual world, but it is certainly not the end of his quest. The island is not the goal; it is the place of preparation. In some cases, such as *The Island of Statues,* where the seeker cannot see beyond the island, the search ends with a mixture of triumph and bitterness. The shift in Yeats's poetry is not so much from emphasis on the goal to the quest itself as it is from the seeker who has faith but no certain knowledge to the seeker who sees more clearly. In the early poetry, the seeker searches through the mists. He knows how he must begin the quest: he must attain the detachment of the island and the wisdom to be found there. The rest of the journey is uncertain.

Yeats's early heroes must reject that part of the world that is corrupt, but they must not reject the world in its entirety. This is the true significance of the statement from *Where There Is Nothing* that is often taken to imply total rejection: " 'We must destroy the World; we must destroy everything that has Law and Number, for where there is nothing, there is God.' "

The full meaning of the statement "where there is nothing, there is God" can be seen in the two poems of Fergus. In "Fergus and the Druid," Fergus states: "But now I have grown nothing, knowing all" (l. 38). If we remember that Fergus was "the poet of the Red Branch cycle, as Oisin was of the Fenian," and that he was "once king of all Ireland but gave up his throne that he might live in peace hunting in the woods" (Yeats's note), and that above all, Fergus was "the king who gave up his kingdom for poetry,"[46] the two poems on Fergus–"Fergus and the Druid" (1892) and "Who Goes with Fergus?" (1899)–add another dimension to the theme of the poet as wanderer and seeker in the early works and show that Yeats's later ideas on the poet-seeker are contained in the earlier poems. These two poems should be taken together, for they complement each other: "Fergus and the Druid" presents Fergus at the time he gives up his kingdom for the wisdom of the Druid, and "Who Goes with Fergus?" reveals Fergus long after his encounter with the Druid, as a symbol for poetic aspiration. The vision that is important here is the nature of the transformation from king to poet, and the significance of that transformation.

In "Fergus and the Druid," Fergus despairs of his kingship, of driving his chariot in "the white border of the murmuring sea"–an image evoking a mood of being on the edge of true existence. Fergus wishes to "be no more a king" and to learn the "dreaming wisdom" of the Druid. A king, according to Fergus, "wastes his blood to be another's dream." Nevertheless, when Fergus attains his knowledge from the "small slate-coloured bag" of the Druid, he attains wisdom, but not happiness. He becomes many things, and nothing:

> I see my life go drifting like a river
> From change to change; I have been many things–
> A green drop in the surge, a gleam of light
> Upon a sword, a fir-tree on a hill,
> An old slave grinding at a heavy quern,
> A king sitting upon a chair of gold–
> And all these things were wonderful and great;
> But now I have grown nothing, knowing all.
> Ah! Druid, Druid, how great webs of sorrow
> Lay hidden in the small slate-coloured thing!
> (ll. 31–40)

The river here is strongly reminiscent of the river of Heraclitus, the state of always becoming, never being. However, these lines express Fergus's point of view. In actuality, Fergus has come close to a state of pure being, but, as a mortal, he cannot bear his all-encompassing state of existence. The earlier versions of this poem make the situation clearer. In the versions printed between 1892 and 1895, Fergus states:

> A wild and foolish labourer is a king
> To do and do and do and never dream.
>
> (ll. 27-28)

When Fergus opens the Druid's bag of dreams and sees his life in a flux of changing existences, he observes:

> But now I have grown nothing, being all. . . .

In the first published version (*The National Observer*, 21 May 1892), the thought of this line was completed by the following lines:

> The sorrows of the world bow down my head,
> And in my heart the daemons and the gods
> Wage an eternal battle, and I feel
> The pain of wounds, the labour of the spear,
> But have no share in loss or victory.

The change from "knowing" to "being" and the explanation of the state of being indicate clearly the true nature of the "great webs of sorrow." In these earlier versions, Fergus does not merely know the life of the world; he has become the world of the natural and the supernatural. He is a part of all being, and all being is a part of him. Nevertheless, his own being is not complete. He feels the pain of life, but he does not share in its results.

Fergus has succeeded, as far as possible, in the attempt to "come clear of the nets of wrong and right," but the nets have been replaced by the webs of sorrow. These two images are very closely connected, both having the meaning of trap and ensnare; they so obviously parallel each other that a similarity or even an identity between the world of man (appealed to in "Into the Twilight") and the world of the Druid and the transformed Fergus is certainly not too far-fetched an interpretation.

In "Who Goes with Fergus?" Fergus is seen in a state of pure being. If the "young man" of the poem goes with Fergus, he will "brood on hopes and fear no more." He will go with a now transcendent Fergus, who

... rules the brazen cars,
And rules the shadows of the wood,
And the white breast of the dim sea
And all dishevelled wandering stars.

(ll. 9-12)

In the first poem Fergus has given up an unsatisfactory life for
an existence of sorrow—Fergus sees his fate as a dreamy, futile
martyrdom. However, in the second poem the martyrdom has a
deeper meaning and a larger significance. We now see Fergus
from a larger view. He has gone through a poetic dark night of
the soul to emerge in the light of true poetic being. He is no
longer on the rim of the sea: he rules the white breast of the
sea. He is not only in the center of life: he controls it.

Thus the two poems on Fergus show the inner progress of the
developing poet, from the physical world of appearance, the
so-called "real world," to the true world of ideal existence.
Again, Yeats has not tried to escape life. With Fergus he enters
life, the eternal world of poetic reality.

The eternal world here, as in "Byzantium," is very closely
allied, supported, and sustained by the physical world: the per-
son who goes with Fergus must "pierce the deep wood's woven
shade, / And dance upon the level shore." And Fergus himself,
as the lines quoted above show, rules over the world of physical
appearances and sensation.

If we consider the points of view of these two poems, another
matter under consideration is made clearer. "Fergus and the
Druid" is dramatic in form, but the reader is more conscious
of Fergus's point of view. The Druid is rather matter-of-fact
in his statements, but he expresses clearly the disillusion with
the spiritual world that has already been mentioned. He describes
his aging body, his uselessness for other humans, and his conscious-
ness that he has failed as a human:

Look on my thin grey hair and hollow cheeks
And on these hands that may not lift the sword,
This body trembling like a wind-blown reed.
No woman's loved me, no man sought my help.

(ll. 23-26)

As we have seen, when he enters the world of the dream, Fergus is overwhelmed by a deep sorrow—suggestive of the awareness of evil in the world of faerie. The partially enlightened point of view is aware of the imperfections of both worlds. Before he opened the bag of dreams, Fergus saw only the imperfection of the world of human affairs. When he acquired Druidic wisdom, he saw the imperfections of both worlds. The beginning seeker, then, is unaware of the disillusion and sorrow that await him.

The point of view in "Who Goes with Fergus?" is more ambiguous. The speaker could be one, like the early Fergus, who aspires to poetic wisdom. The facts in the poem, however, seem to indicate a more abstract, omniscient speaker. The fact that the identity of the speaker is uncertain may be important, for the sorrow is absent in this poem. The ideal represented by Fergus is certainly that which Fergus expected to find when he sought out the Druid. If the speaker in the poem is an aspiring young poet, he does not see Fergus's poetic existence as Fergus himself sees it. If the speaker does represent an omniscient overview, then Fergus has attained the goal of the seeker. At any rate, the very fact that Fergus can be envisioned in this manner indicates that the hope of the seeker can be realized, for the goal does exist in vision; but the ambiguity of the speaker reveals the uncertainty of the seeker while he is in the act of searching. The quest, then, becomes an act of faith, and the disillusion experienced along the way becomes a testing of that faith.

The two Fergus poems show the search at its simplest: Fergus seeks the "dreaming wisdom" of the Druid; it is given him; he passes through a period of disillusion in the initial stage of union with all life; and finally he achieves a form of poetic beatification. Fergus renounces his throne to seek the wisdom of the Druid; symbolically, he leaves the cares of the materialistic world to dedicate himself to poetry.

In the longer poems, the search is more detailed: the seeker is summoned and leaves the land for an island; he leaves the countinghouse world for a place that is earthly yet isolated from the world in the same way that Fergus leaves his kingship to follow the Druid among the rocks. At this stage, the seeker is in the physical world, yet he has left behind the complexities that modern civilization forces upon him. Somewhere along the route he meets the possessor of wisdom—one who already comprehends the reality of the physical and the spiritual. The journey is now beginning. The many islands found in Yeats's early poetry—or sometimes a wooded place—become a testing-ground or place of novitiate for the seeker. Sometimes, as in *The Seeker,* the wanderer meets with disaster at this point. At other times, as in *The Island of Statues,* the search ends at the island on a note of success tinged with hints of sorrow and death. When the search goes beyond the island, as in *The Shadowy Waters,* the poet-seeker heads for the open and misty sea. Throughout his poetry, Yeats is aware that the search does not end with the island, yet we are often presented with a seeker who (perhaps like Yeats himself) cannot at present see the way beyond.

The environment of the search is the world of transition. The seeker often feels that he is somewhere between the natural and the supernatural, and metaphorically he is pictured as such. Yet the mists, the obscurity, the lyrical, trancelike language, the presence of the landscape and the small creatures of earth, show him to be in the world of the dream, the world in which realities of both natural and supernatural become mingled, the world of vision leading to the true reality of being.

CHAPTER THREE

TWO COMPONENTS OF THE QUEST

THE ISLAND AND THE POSSESSOR OF WISDOM

THE ISLAND

> Shy one, shy one,
> Shy one of my heart,
> She moves in the firelight
> Pensively apart.
>
> She carries in the dishes,
> And lays them in a row.
> To an isle in the water
> With her would I go.
>
> ("To an Isle in the Water," ll. 1-8)

These two stanzas, apparently trivial in subject, treat an important component of the poetic search—the island. On first consideration, this poem, "To an Isle in the Water," appears to be a lesser statement of "The Lake Isle of Innisfree." Both poems evoke a mood of quietness, simplicity, and retreat. The detail of dishes laid in a row is even reminiscent of the nine bean rows of Innisfree. However, when one examines Yeats's concern with islands, ranging from brief references in short lyrics such as "To an Isle in the Water" and "The Lake Isle of Innisfree" to longer poems such as *The Wanderings of Oisin,* in which the hero travels with Niamh to the three islands, and to the poetic drama *The Island of Statues,* in which the enchanted island is the center of

the action, the island—the lake island, the island in the water—
becomes a recurrent theme, a leitmotif, throughout Yeats's early
poetry. The importance of the island is suggested in the 1906
version of *The Shadowy Waters:*

> *Aibric.* And if that happiness be more than dreams,
> More than the froth, the feather, the dust-whirl,
> The crazy nothing that I think it is,
> It shall be in the country of the dead,
> If there be such a country.
>
> *Dectora.*   No, not there
> But in some island where the life of the world
> Leaps upward, as if all the streams o' the world
> Had run into one fountain.
>   (ll. 554–561)

The island in these lines is clearly of more significance than a
small island in Lough Gill that became the subject of a poem
inspired by the writings of Thoreau and yearning for home.[47]
    There is a legitimate question that must be posed here: Can
there be any real connection between the small lake island and
the supernatural islands of *The Shadowy Waters* or *The Wander-
ings of Oisin?* Are both types of island a version of the "place
apart," the place of withdrawal necessary in the pastoral? Since
the island is used in so many of the poems directly involved with
the poet-seeker, it is logical to examine Yeats's treatments of
the islands to see if some overall pattern emerges. The island in
Yeats always seems to have a direct connection with life. This
connection is established either through such small details as
the dishes, the candles, and the rabbit in "To an Isle in the
Water" or through direct statement, as in the lines quoted
above from *The Shadowy Waters.* No matter how remote the
location, the connotations of *island*—isolation, solitude, refuge,
in many poems the place of contact with the supernatural—are
delicately balanced with the reality of Innisfree, the small lake
island in County Sligo, If, through a detailed examination, one
compares "The Lake Isle of Innisfree" with Yeats's other uses
of the island, the poem, in its direct connection to the specific
place, emerges as a clear prototype for the island in Yeats. By a

strong descriptive resemblance to Innisfree itself, or by a per-
haps more tenuous relationship with the poem, even those islands
that appear the most exotic retain something of the atmosphere
of truth and reality. The clear statement of this lyric serves to
clarify and inform many of Yeats's poems, both earlier and later,
in relation to the artistic function of the island.

"The Lake Isle of Innisfree" has been overanthologized and
overdiscussed to such an extent that it is often overlooked in
serious discussions of Yeats; in a letter to Sturge Moore in 1907,
Yeats called it "that damned Innisfree."[48] Yet this exquisite
lyric is a perfect example of Yeats's technique in evoking the
mood commonly referred to as "the Celtic Twilight." In this
poem, Yeats reveals the strong influence of Romanticism on his
early work (the first printing was in 1890) and displays his artist-
ry in taking the moods and thoughts of the Romantics and mak-
ing of them something entirely his own. In this poem, as every
high-school student knows, Yeats speaks of nostalgia for primitive
isolation in nature—back to Walden, back to Eden, or what you
will; the story of the water-jet in the London shop window is
familar to all of Yeats's readers. Nevertheless, this treatment of
what many readers consider an overworked theme emerges as a
new and valid work of art. It would be a mistake to dismiss
"Innisfree" because of its familiarity. In this poem Yeats has
achieved a perfect blending of sound and sense. The consummate
artistry displayed here places this poem at the peak of his early
work. The balance of "Innisfree" and its virtually perfect struc-
ture combine to make the poem itself a symbolic island, indicat-
ing the apparent perfection and unity of the physical island that
inspired the poem.

In the first place, the poem is grounded in reality. Innisfree is
just as real as Walden Pond or the tower Yeats purchased. Any-
one can go there. If this is Eden, it is after the Fall. If Innisfree
represents escape, it is the escape of the seeking hermit. Yeats
does retreat from the modern world of materialism and industry,
but he does so in order to find a true world of meaning, a world
in which man lives a unified existence, and not a world that he
tries to conquer by means of the latest hydroelectric scheme.
The specifics of the nine bean rows, the small cabin of clay and
wattles, and the beehive in the first stanza, the cricket and the

linnets in the second, all keep the poem and its vision within the realm of the concrete world of man.

A comparison of Yeats's allusions to islands reveals a definite pattern of evocation. The island is usually seen from the perspective of the shore or of the more involved world existing outside it. Like Innisfree, the island is a focal point for the longings and dreams of the seekers, and it thus becomes an integral part of the search. Many of Yeats's seekers are seen upon the shore, which evokes ideas of the end of the land and the beginning of the sea journey. The shore is the end and the beginning. The Indian, in "The Indian upon God," begins his meditations on the edge of the water:

> I passed along the water's edge below the humid trees,
> My spirit rocked in evening light, the rushes round
>   my knees,
> My spirit rocked in sleep and sighs; and saw the
>   moorfowl pace. . . .
>   (ll. 1–3)

The pensive, bittersweet words of "Ephemera" are uttered on "the lone border of the lake" (ll. 5, 17). Here again "Fergus and the Druid" is pertinent. Fergus's despair is being a proud king. He drives his chariot on the edge of the sea and still feels the crown upon his head. On the shore one is still governed by material things; the island is the next step of the journey, the haven beyond the shore—perhaps a place of preparation and meditation in which one loses the false reality of the world of materialism and finds the true reality of Being.

Such generalizations are based on the striking similarity among the islands that appear in Yeats's early work. A few examples will reveal the solidity of the evidence. In *The Island of Statues,* Almintor tells of his journey in a magic boat to "The lake-embosomed isle" (I, iii. 60). In *Mosada,* Mosada will summon a Phantom "Whose dwelling was a tree-wrapt island" (I, 79). "The Indian to His Love" centers around an island:

> The island dreams under the dawn
> And great boughs drop tranquillity. . . .
>   (ll. 1–2)

The first version of "He tells of the Perfect Beauty" addresses the "daughter of the Island of Woods"; and in "The Withering of the Boughs," the poet tells of a fairy island in the lake. "The Stolen Child" refers specifically to Innisfree, which lies just offshore from Sleuth Wood:

> Where dips the rocky highland
> Of Sleuth Wood in the lake,
> There lies a leafy island
> Where flapping herons wake. . . .
> (ll. 1-4)

"The Stolen Child" reveals a total mixture of the natural and the supernatural: the supernatural in the fairy life and the possible reference in lines 6-7 (the "faery vats, / Full of berries") to the enchanted quicken tree, which, Yeats tells us in a note (*The Bookman*, May 1893), once grew on Innisfree; the natural in the leaves, the herons, and the water-rats. The island thus becomes the meeting point of the two worlds. Still, however, it is no Eden. It is the home of evil and of good. As we see in "The Danaan Quicken Tree," the tranquillity of Innisfree has its sinister counterpart:

> Beloved, hear my bitter tale!—
> Now making busy with the oar,
> Now flinging loose the slanting sail,
> I hurried from the woody shore,
> And plucked small fruits on Innisfree.
> (Ah, mournful Danaan quicken tree!)
> (ll. 1-6)

The red berries of the quicken tree

> . . . are a poison to all men
> and meat to the Aslauga Shee.
> (ll. 16-17)

This is one of the clearest contrasts in Yeats between the two worlds: the food of the fairies is poison to men. In *The Island of Statues*, the Enchantress on the island says to Naschina:

> now thou hast grown kind,
> And thou wilt stay. All thought of what they find
> In the far world will vanish from thy mind,
> Till thou rememberest only how the sea
> Has fenced us round for all eternity.
> (II, iii, 91–95)

All of Yeats's islands, both natural and supernatural, have this function. Even though Oisin's islands can be identified with the legendary islands of the Immortals in the west and thus suggest the attainment of a goal of happiness, or perhaps the blessedness found by Saint Brendan in his voyage to islands in the west, Oisin returns disillusioned to an Ireland he no longer knows. The island is not the goal of the search: Yeats realizes that he cannot remain on Innisfree. The island is, however, one remove from the shore, and he who attains it becomes ready to embark on the major part of his quest. The islands, then, both natural and supernatural, become the place of withdrawal of the pastoral tradition. The men of the world—Oisin and the others—do return to the activity of humanity; or, if there is no return, there is no eternal peace.

THE POSSESSOR OF WISDOM

Often involved in Yeats's poetic search is a mysterious figure who can be called in general terms the possessor of wisdom. The figure is as elusive as Matthew Arnold's Scholar Gypsy, combining mystery with strange hints of immortality. The seekers are conscious of the existence of a world beyond this world, a supernatural realm that seems to contain the wisdom they are seeking. They are drawn to the search by voices from the supernatural, and their quest into the unknown often leads them to a figure who, they think, possesses the knowledge of enlightenment. In the early poetry, however, the search does not lead to certain enlightenment, and it is not until *Baile and Aillinn,* written in 1902, that the seekers achieve happiness. The journey is dangerous and fraught with mystery; the figure, when encountered, leads to disappointment and sometimes death. Part of the enigma lies in the fact of the human condition. The seekers are mortal, and cannot fully understand the meaning they have encountered.

It may be of significance that Aengus, in *Baile and Aillinn,* appears as an evil figure, a "gaunt old man," who leads the two lovers to happiness after their death. Fergus is disappointed with the wisdom of the Druid; he does not find contentment until he achieves immortality. In *The Wanderings of Oisin,* Niamh speaks these words:

> "O wandering Oisin, the strength of the bell-branch is naught,
> For there moves alive in your fingers the fluttering sadness
> of earth."
> (III, 123-124)

Earth casts a veil that clouds the seeker's vision; his perspective is thus limited by mundane appearances. The cosmic view, an overall comprehension of the universe, seems to be beyond his grasp.

This, then, is the problem with which Yeats is wrestling: How does one pierce the veil and achieve enlightenment? Can one attain enlightenment in this life? If man can sense that such wisdom exists, that there is such a thing as enlightenment, is it not conceivable that man could reach this state? Yeats was aware of stories, both ancient and modern, concerning enlightened beings. Madame Blavatsky and her followers spoke of the "Masters" who give the wisdom of the universe to certain humans who are capable of understanding it (such as Madame Blavatsky).

In his readings Yeats was intrigued by the magician figure—the legendary man who had attained immortality and immortal wisdom. This interest is revealed especially in his very early poetry. In the *Autobiographies* covering the years 1887–1891, Yeats says:

> . . . my mind gave itself to gregarious Shelley's dream of a young man, his hair blanched with sorrow, studying philosophy in some lonely tower, or of his old man, master of all human knowledge, hidden from human sight in some shell-strewn cavern of the Mediterranean shore.[49]

Yeats quotes a passage from *Hellas,* in which the dwelling place of Ahasuerus and his inaccessibility are described, and in which the young man Mahmud expresses the desire to be one of the few who "win the desired communion" with the immortal man of wisdom. In his poetry, Yeats adapts the idea of the intermediary between the two worlds and presents him from the viewpoint of the seeker of wisdom. It is for this reason that the possessor of wisdom is never a clearly delineated figure. The fact of his existence is certain, but his outline is hazed in mystery.

The problem of the poet's relation to time and the shortness of life has already been discussed in connection with the environment of the search. However, more needs to be said here concerning the possessor of wisdom and time. Throughout the early poetry we find Druids and enchantresses who, by implication at least, are immortal. Nevertheless, the immortality of even these semilegendary figures is brought into question. In the short dramatic poem "Time and the Witch Vivien," which was printed in *The Wanderings of Oisin and Other Poems* (1889), Yeats deals directly with the relationship between the possessor of wisdom and time. The witch Vivien—the same who imprisoned Merlin in the tree—is seen in a large pillared room with a fountain (symbolic of life?), her magical instruments very much in evidence in one corner. As the poem begins, she is staring into the fountain, contemplating her beauty and musing upon her magical powers. Time enters. She plays dice with him and loses, then gains for herself a second chance at chess, hoping to defeat him with her wits since chance has not favored her. She feels confident because she has outsmarted Merlin. However, again she loses: Time checks her three times before mate. Having lost, she dies. The Enchantress in *The Island of Statues,* who has "seen a thousand seasons ebb and flow" (II, iii, 229), dies when Naschina, the shepherdess destined by old fable to find the flower of wizardry, fulfills the conditions of the prophecy. The condition, ironically, is that the shepherdess cannot succeed unless she finds someone to die for her. In her turn, Naschina will attain immortality, a state of existence described to her by the Enchantress in these lines:

> Thou shalt outlive thine amorous happy time,
> And dead as are the lovers of old rime
> Shall be the hunter-lover of thy youth.
> Yet even more, through all thy days of ruth,
> Shall grow thy beauty and thy dreamless truth. . . .
> (II, iii, 203-7)

Naschina cannot anticipate a state of bliss. She will lose and long
for transitory earthly things, and, significantly, the truth she will
know will be dreamless. The sadness of immortality and the con-
sciousness of time are echoed throughout the play, even in the
"happy" ending. The power of the evil Enchantress is broken;
Almintor, the seeker-figure of the drama, has achieved his quest
and is made king of the Arcadians: on the surface, an idyllic con-
clusion to a frothy Arcadian play. There is more than gilding
here, however. These are Almintor's final words, addressed to
the now immortal Naschina:

> Until we die within the charmed ring
> Of these star-shuddering skies, you are the queen.

After these words, "the rising moon casts the shadows of Almin-
tor and the Sleepers far across the grass. Close by Almintor's
side, Naschina is standing, shadowless." Thus the play ends.

In these early poetic efforts we might expect the optimism of
a young poet to deal with Arcadian or legendary material in a
more superficial manner. Yet here we see the same ambiguous,
bittersweet consciousness of life and mortality in relation to im-
mortality that is found in the later poems; in fact, we find the
"elegiac feeling" of Arcadia noted by Erwin Panofsky in his
essay "Et in Arcadia Ego."[50] One could perhaps moralize at
this point and say that the eternity of art is not an eternity of
bliss, but Yeats is not preaching sermons, certainly not sermons
on obvious facts. The point is that in the poetic dream one does
not and cannot escape from the "real world"—the real world, in
truth, is that of poetry and life, of poetry in life. There is a ten-
sion between two worlds, but they both exist simultaneously
and one is not denied for the other. In "The Host of the Air,"
O'Driscoll dreams of his bride who has been taken away by the
fairies:

> He heard while he sang and dreamed
> A piper piping away,
> And never was piping so sad,
> And never was piping so gay.

> And he saw young men and young girls
> Who danced on a level place,
> And Bridget his bride among them,
> With a sad and a gay face.
>
> (ll. 9-16)

The fairies try to charm him with bread and wine, for one who
eats of fairy food is glamoured and stolen. Bridget draws him to
a game of cards to keep him from harm. As the ballad ends:

> O'Driscoll scattered the cards
> And out of his dream awoke:
> Old men and young men and young girls
> Were gone like a drifting smoke;
>
> But he heard high up in the air
> A piper piping away,
> And never was piping so sad,
> And never was piping so gay.
>
> (ll. 37-44)

The supernatural world in this ballad has two ambiguities. First,
it is both sad and gay, as the world of man is sad and gay. Second,
the reality and the dream are seen in the last two stanzas to exist
simultaneously. O'Driscoll awakes, and still hears the music. The
dream is quite real: there is no storybook awakening.

In the early Arcadian poetry, as we have seen, the possessor
of wisdom is shadowy and often demonic, appearing in the
guise of an enchantress. In *The Island of Statues,* Naschina, the
shepherdess, outlines to Almintor the romantic ideal of the
search: A knight will "prove his love" on a world-circling quest
for a dragon with whom he will fight from dawn to dusk, or he
will

> . . . seek enchanter old,
> Who sits in lonely splendour, . . .
> And they will war. . . .
>
> (I, i. 162-164)

Almintor considers himself upon "a most fearful quest" (I, ii, 31), and he is lured farther by a Voice who claims to have been present when Eve sinned; who wandered and sang "round the tree" in Eden as it now sings "follow" (I, ii, 60–69). The Lilith-like implications are obvious: the Voice is temptation, leading Almintor to possible evil. The association with Eve and the tree hint toward the acquisition of knowledge and the fall from innocence. The Voice leads Almintor to the island home of the Enchantress, who has snared numerous seekers throughout history and turned them into statues of stone.

Almintor is now said to be "evil-starred" (I, ii, 84); and he does fall from innocence. He leaves the innocent world of Arcady for the fairy island, where he does find victory but also deceit and awareness of death. He defeats the Enchantress and frees the charmed seekers, some of whom have been sleeping since before Troy fell, but the wisdom he finds is the knowledge that one day he will die.

In *The Seeker,* the old Knight comes to the land of the shepherds after "threescore years of dream-led wandering" (l. 16). A voice has led him to this land and to a wood that represents the absence of life. The shepherds warn him that "no shepherd foot has ever dared its depths" (l. 32) and that "the very squirrel dies that enters there" (l. 33). The wood is death itself, but the Knight is compelled to enter.

In the forest he finds a ruined palace, and amid the ruins a shadowy motionless Figure. He implores the Figure to speak, but before she speaks the Knight feels himself dying. He moves closer, and a sudden light bursts over the Figure:

> A bearded witch, her sluggish head low bent
> On her broad breast! Beneath her withered brows
> Shine dull unmoving eyes. . . .
>
> (ll. 72–74)

The poem ends as follows: The Knight, upon seeing the horror of the Figure asks

> . . . What thing art thou?
> I sought thee not. . . .
> (ll. 74–75)

The Figure answers that men call her Infamy, but she knows not what she is. Addressing the Knight as "lover," she states that it is her voice that summoned him. She raises a mirror, in which he sees shadowed his face and form. He falls, hears again her voice—*the* voice—and dies. The mysterious voice has led the old knight to his death; the Figure remains enigmatic. She is called Infamy by men, but, significantly, she cannot name herself. At the conclusion of the poem, she takes on some of the qualities of the demon lover, some of the qualities of the Sirens or the Lorelei. The important fact is that she is the possessor of the voice, and the voice remains unchanged.

In *Mosada,* the enchantress figure possesses many of the same qualities, but her agency in evil is indirect. Mosada summons the "Phantom fair" (l. 76), whose actions she describes:

> . . . There in a dell,
> A lily-blanchèd place, she sat and sang,
> And in her singing wove around her head
> White lilies, and her song flew forth afar
> Along the sea; and many a man grew hushed
> In his own house or 'mong the merchants grey,
> Hearing the far-off singing guile, and groaned,
> And manned an argosy and sailing died.
>   (I, 82-91)

Mosada feels what she believes to be the presence of the Phantom, but the door is opened to admit the Officers of the Inquisition. The Phantom herself does not bring death to Mosada—though, like the Sirens, she has lured many men to their deaths. It is Mosada's act of attempting to summon beings from another world that causes her to be tried by the Inquisition. Though the reality of the Phantom is never in doubt, she never appears in the play; she remains an enigma. From one point of view, the human, Mosada, almost becomes the unsuccessful enchantress. There is no evidence of the oncoming vision but her own statement, and at the end she takes upon herself the powers of life and death by taking a fatal dose of poison. Thus Mosada engineers for herself the same lure and the same fatal end experienced by the Knight in *The Seeker.*

In the Irish poetry, the lure of the voice and the mysterious possessor of wisdom lose the similarity with the Sirens and Lorelei and much of the evil connotations of these mythological figures. In *The Wanderings of Oisin,* Saint Patrick, the representative of the new, drab, nonheroic culture, accuses Oisin of three centuries of "dalliance with a demon thing" (I, 3–4). Niamh may be a demon to Saint Patrick and to the poets he heard sing of her, but she is not evil to Oisin:

> A pearl-pale, high-born lady, who rode
> On a horse with bridle of findrinny;
> And like a sunset were her lips,
> A stormy sunset on doomed ships;
> A citron colour gloomed in her hair,
> But down to her feet white vesture flowed,
> And with the glimmering crimson glowed
> Of many a figured embroidery;
> And it was bound with a pearl-pale shell
> That wavered like the summer streams,
> As her soft bosom rose and fell.
>   (I, 20–30)

According to Saint Patrick, Oisin is "still wrecked among heathen dreams" (I, 31). The only hint of evil in this description of Niamh, which immediately precedes Saint Patrick's pronouncement, is in the lines: "A stormy sunset on doomed ships; / A citron colour gloomed in her hair." The words *stormy, doomed, gloomed,* placed in positions of stress, connote a sense of foreboding destruction rather than malignant evil. Niamh lured him away from the world, but she cannot return him to the heroic age. Not only is Oisin immune to the spells of the bell-branch; he is also disappointed by the three islands to which Niamh leads him:

> And then lost Niamh murmured, "Love, we go
> To the Island of Forgetfulness, for lo!
> The Islands of Dancing and of Victories
> Are empty of all power."
>   "And which of these
> Is the Island of Content?"
>   "None know," she said;
> And on my bosom laid her weeping head.
>   (II, 245–250)

In the 1889 version, the Island of Content is known as the Isle of Youth. Niamh's answer to the question in both verions is the same: "None know."

Book II of *The Wanderings of Oisin* ends in sadness and uncertainty; Book III, the final book, ends in disappointment. When Oisin touches the ground of Ireland, he attains his full age. He elects to join the Fenian heroes, whether they be in hell or at feast, rather than accept the Christian salvation offered him by Saint Patrick, for salvation would mean eternal separation from the pagan heroes. His search with Niamh has been unsuccessful: he must leave the shadowy, vague existence offered by Niamh and return to the land he knows, where Maeve's cairn broods over the countryside. He finds, however, that his old world has vanished and that he must accept a new world on Saint Patrick's terms. Saint Patrick, the possessor of the new wisdom, has conquered and destroyed the world of the heroes.

After presenting the problem of modern Ireland—the loss of the heroic age—in *The Wanderings of Oisin,* Yeats's search shifts from the regaining of the past to the attainment of the eternal, which contains the natural and the supernatural, the past, present, and the future.

One figure Yeats uses to link temporal man with the world of the eternal is the Druid. The Druids, mysterious personages from the almost legendary past, are perfectly suited to Yeats's purpose. The Druid is a native Celtic figure and is associated directly with poetry, wisdom, ritual, and power. Yeats's sources of knowledge about the Irish past provide him with a poetic Irish figure analogous to Madame Blavatsky's Tibetan "Masters."

Virginia Moore poses the question "What Celtic specialists did he [Yeats] read after O'Grady, during the period when, working on the ritual for his Irish mysteries, he was concerned with Druids as repositories of an ancient esoteric knowledge?" She finds the answer through "frequent allusions" to John Rhŷs, Douglas Hyde, and Arbois de Jubainville.[51] To give an idea of what Yeats probably read about the Druids, I will quote a short passage from Douglas Hyde, who gives an account of the Druids in *A Literary History of Ireland from Earliest Times to the Present Day,* which was first published in 1894. Dr. Hyde states that little is known of the Druids, except that they are mentioned from the earliest times and are associated with kings and poets. Dr. Hyde observes:

Kings were sometimes Druids, so were poets. It is a word which seems to me to have been, perhaps from the first, used with great laxity and great latitude.

We find a very minute account in the tenth-century glossary of King Cormac as to how a poet performed Incantations with his idols. The word "poet" is here apparently equivalent to druid, as the word "druid" like the Latin *vates* is frequently a synonym for "poet."[52]

Dr. Hyde then quotes from the tenth-century glossary of King Cormac explaining the incantation *Imbas Forosnai*, in which the poet, after the proper rituals and invocations, seeks "whatsoever thing he wishes to discover" in sleep.[53] Dr. Hyde also observes that "another phase of the druidic character seems to have been that he was looked upon as an intermediary between man and the invisible powers."[54]

The Druid, then, has a direct and important connection with the significance of sleep and the dream. Consequently, such a line as "He has thrown a druid dream upon the air" (*Shadowy Waters,* 1900 version, l. 237) assumes an added significance. The reference to Druid is not merely a colorful evocation; it calls upon associations with the power of poetry and the power of ritual in addition to the power of the mysterious magic of the Druids. In addition, according to one of Douglas Hyde's sources, the Druids had strong earthly power:

"Those philosophers," (says Diodorus Siculus, a Greek writer of the Augustine age, speaking of the Druids) "like the lyric poets called bards, have a great authority both in affairs of peace and war; friends and enemies listen to them. Also when the two armies are in the presence of one another, and swords drawn and spears couched, they throw themselves in the midst of the combatants and appease them as though they were charming wild beasts."[55]

Upon first consideration, the Druid seems so ideally suited for Yeats that it is surprising he did not make more use of the figure. The Druid is used more often as an adjective ("a Druid land, a Druid tune") than as a character; thus, the Druid is present more often in the background than in the foreground. In the poems written in or before 1906, including variant readings, and on three occasions (once in a variant) in which the word is used twice in the same line for emphasis, *Druid* appears twenty-three times as an adjective, six times as a noun, and *Druids* is used seven times.

Druids, or druid-like figures, however, are more important in Yeats's early poetry than these statistics would indicate. Druids or references to them are scattered throughout the poems on Irish subject matter written between 1889 and 1906. The reader cannot help but sense their presence. For Yeats, the world of the Irish hero is also the world of their gods and their Druids. The Druid—as an integral part of the ancient world, as a priest, a poet, and a white magician—becomes, in the Irish poetry, essential to the Weltanschauung of the poet-seeker.

"Cuchulain's Fight with the Sea" does not present the Druids as part of a poetic quest. This poem is important in connection with the possessor of wisdom, however, for it shows the Druids in their historical environment, possessing and using the power that tradition attributes to them. To protect himself and his company from being slain by Cuchulain, Conchubar, "the subtlest of all men" (1. 75), instructs his Druids to chant in Cuchulain's ear "'delusions magical, / That he may fight the horses of the sea' " (ll. 80–81). The Druids chant for three days. Cuchulain then rises up, stares on the horses of the sea, hears the cars of battle and his own name called. He then goes out and fights "with the invulnerable tide" (1. 86). This is the power of poetry, ritual, and the dream.

In the 1889–1906 body of poetry, the Druid replaces the evil or quasi-evil enchantress. He, as the possessor of wisdom, is still a mysterious figure, but his connotations are good. The demonic figure is slipping out of view, and appears only as the rather strange being in *The Wanderings of Oisin:*

> And on the runnel's stony and bare edge
> A dusky demon dry as a withered sedge
> Swayed, crooning to himself an unknown tongue:
> In a sad revelry he sang and swung
> Bacchant and mournful. . . .
>
> (II, 157–161)

The demon is defeated by the sword of Manannan, significantly called in some of the earlier versions "the druid sword of Manannan."

In relation to the possessor of wisdom, *The Wanderings of Oisin* can be seen as a transition poem. Such allusions as "the druid sword of Manannan" indicate that there are higher powers in the form of mediators between two worlds, yet these powers do not appear directly. Instead, Yeats presents us with personages who are ineffectual for Oisin. Saint Patrick is a mediator for the Christian world; his presence spells death to the poetic world of the hero. Niamh, from the world of faerie, leads Oisin on a fruitless quest. All the power of the gods—even Aengus, who sometimes appears as a possessor of wisdom—and the power of the mystic bell-branch become sterile when applied to Oisin, who is too much tainted by the material world. Oisin never confronts a figure with the power of the Druid.

Oisin does confront Aengus in Book I of *The Wanderings of Oisin,* on the Island of the Immortals. Niamh requests that she and Oisin be taken

> . . . to the hall
> Where Aengus dreams, from sun to sun,
> A Druid dream of the end of days
> When stars are to wane and the world be done.
> (I, 217-220)

Aengus appears in the following guise:

> A beautiful young man dreamed within
> A house of wattles, clay, and skin;
> One hand upheld his beardless chin,
> And one a sceptre flashing out
> Wild flames of red and gold and blue. . . .
> (I, 248-252)

Aengus speaks of the joy of this land, of the contrast between the timelessness of the Immortals, of the heroic courage of men of old, and the careworn hearts of the present day. He then falls into a "Druid swoon" (l. 289), and the Immortals break into a wild dance.

The joy of the Immortals, however, is permeated with an undertone of mortal sorrow. They cannot bear to hear Oisin sing of human joy; they are continually conscious that they do not fear "the grey wandering osprey sorrow." They are too conscious of avoiding sorrow to be truly happy. Oisin, being mortal, can experience the happiness of the Immortals—such as it is—only temporarily. Reminded of the Fenians, and of the "ancient sorrow of men" (l. 381), Oisin leaves. Aengus has no lasting effect on Oisin. His power, and eventually his land, appear sterile and artificial. Aengus and the Immortals are satisfied with his wisdom; for Oisin, it is insufficient.

After *The Wanderings of Oisin,* the possessor of wisdom (now often identified as a Druid or Aengus) becomes more like the solitary man of contemplation mentioned by Yeats in "The Symbolism of Poetry" (1900):

Solitary men in moments of contemplation receive, as I think, the creative impulse from the lowest of the Nine Hierarchies, and so make and unmake mankind, and even the world itself, for does not "the eye altering alter all?"[56]

A prototype of the solitary man is found in the short story "Where There Is Nothing, There Is God," from *The Secret Rose.* In this story a mysterious, humble beggar, with ragged beard and matted hair, clad in tattered clothes, comes to a small group of Irish monks. He looks at them all with "mild, ecstatic eyes" and asks for shelter. Later he asks for work and accepts the humblest tasks with willingness. The old man is found to be a worker of miracles through prayer. There is a child, Olioll, known for his stupidity. Suddenly the child gains wisdom. Brother Dove, Olioll's teacher, follows him to find the nature of the miracle. He follows Olioll to the beggar. When he arrives, he finds himself to be in a holy place, in which the birds and animals are not afraid of man. Olioll opens the book, tries to read, and cries when he cannot. The beggar comforts him until he falls asleep. Then the beggar prays, Olioll is wrapped in a light which "broke out of the air," and Brother Dove smells the breath of roses. At the end of Brother Dove's account of this incident, the abbot identifies the old beggar as "Aengus the Lover of God, and the first of those who have gone to live in the wild places and among the

wild beasts." Ten years before, Aengus had retired to the forest,
but his fame attracted many thousands to his cell. He abandoned
his hermitage, and for the past nine years he has been wandering.
Aengus has reached the end of his search and is now a leader for
others. The abbot states:

"Let us go to him and bow down before him; for at last, after long seeking,
he has found the nothing that is God; and bid him lead us in the pathway
he has trodden."[57]

Thus the possessor of wisdom is identified with the first
seeker, and Aengus, the pagan god of love, now the Lover of
God, has brought wisdom to a primitive Christian monastic
community. This, perhaps, hints at the fusion or synthesis Yeats
was trying to attain for modern Ireland. Unlike *The Wanderings
of Oisin,* in which, except for Oisin's courage, the Christian order
has defeated the pagan world, here the two worlds become fused,
and each helps the other. Significantly, though, the wisdom comes
from Aengus, and those who receive it are simple and peasant-
like enough to comprehend it. Again unlike Oisin, Olioll's mind
contains "nothing from the world." The boy has the ignorance
of innocence; the seeker, like the enlightened Taoist, must attain
the knowledge that lies beyond the conceptions and intellectual
abstractions of worldly knowledge and become like Fergus, who
has "grown nothing, knowing all."

Aengus, here in a Christian guise, has rejected the pride of
the materialistic world and has found "the nothing that is God"
in the world of animals and trees. He has become simple like the
animals themselves, but he has not rejected life. He has found
wisdom in this world, and he returns to men with the fruits of
his experience. In this story Yeats presents in prose the character
often referred to or alluded to in the poems, the character who
has attained the goal of the seekers: the man who has rejected
the false world of gain, greed, and corruption in order to reach
the true world, a fusion of the spiritual and the physical. Aengus
does not escape to a never-never land, nor does he remain in the
forest permanently. He has found the Land of Heart's Desire,
and it now exists within him. Aengus, like Fergus in "Who Goes
with Fergus?" has become the Master who can lead others along

the way. Since Aengus is seen only from the point of view of others, he appears a tranquil, holy man. We should not forget, however, the view expressed in "Fergus and the Druid." That poem, as we have seen, shows the possessor of wisdom—and the seeker—not as a man who has escaped into a state of tranquillity, but as one who has taken on a greater burden. The cares and sorrows are greater than the troubles of ordinary life because they transcend the mundane. The tranquillity of the possessor of true wisdom is but an appearance. He has not rejected this world; he has accepted more than this world.

CHAPTER FOUR

THE SEEKER AND THE QUEST

THE SEEKER

In Yeats's early poetry, the poet-seeker exists progressively in three locales: Arcadia, India, and Ireland. Yeats's treatment of the seeker in these three poetic settings not only reveals the development of his poetic technique into an individualized voice; it also shows the development of the poet-seeker—however archetypal one may wish to see him—as a character of Yeats's own making, a multifaceted character reflecting in his many personae the complexity of Yeats's own artistic concern.

In Yeats's early poetry, the poet-seeker cannot be isolated into any one prototype, except in the way that a composite of norms can become the "normal" human being. Until Yeats uses the singular first-person pronoun in some of the poems about the rose and in his later poetry (and even here there is much room for argument), the poet-seeker is not one person but many. The Arcadian, Almintor; the Irish pagan hero, Oisin; the shadowy Forgael; and Fergus, who is often more an image than a person: these are a few of the varied guises of the seeker. Again, the poet-seeker is often present through mood rather than in person, as in such poems as "The Unappeasable Host." In order to understand Yeats's poetic quest, it becomes necessary to examine the various facets of the poet-seeker as he appears in the settings of Arcadia, idealized India, and Ireland, and to consider the question of his true identity.

It is well known that Yeats was drawn to the idea of "Unity of Being." He was concerned philosophically and psychologically with this idea, which embraces the union of self, soul, civilization, and culture into one harmonious whole. The search for unity of being is the poetic search in its totality, for in the state of unity the living artist creates the living work. The integrated self and the integrated culture will produce a universal and timeless art.

Very early in his career, Yeats was interested in the condition of the self in its relationship with its cultural environment. He sometimes saw man as running from himself, using the tasks appropriate to him in a flight from the self. Yeats wrote four lines that appeared in the *Dublin University Review* in 1886 under the title "Life" and later as the first quatrain in *Quatrains and Aphorisms:*

> The child who chases lizards in the grass,
> The sage who deep in nature delves,
> The preacher watching for the ill hour to pass—
> All these are souls who fly from their dread selves.

In his biography, Hone gives the following account of an early version of *The Shadowy Waters,* as the young Yeats told the story to George Russell while they were both still at the Art School. Forgael is a "wanderer striving to escape from himself." He suddenly comes upon a galley, in which there is a woman of great beauty. Thinking that love might be the means of escape from himself, he casts a magic spell upon the woman, Dectora. He finds, however, that the love is "but the empty shadow of himself"; he removes ("unrolls") the spell and continues on alone, to seek the "world of the immortals."[58]

This early concern with the flight from the self is not explicitly voiced by Yeats elsewhere in the early poetry. Yet, even the small amount of evidence cited here (especially if considered in the light of his later theories of the mask and the self) shows that Yeats was very early concerned with the identity and integrity of the individual. The later seekers seem more integrated within themselves, if not with their environment. Yeats often examines the individual in a search for unity in his own being; he presents us with persons conscious of a certain fragmentation, motivated by a desire for union within themselves.

When we discuss the fragmentation of the inner being of the poet-seeker, we tread on shaky ground. It is true that Yeats was familiar with theories such as the Platonic conception of the two halves of the soul, and that the union of Forgael and Dectora in *The Shadowy Waters* seems to be a union of the two halves of the person, but Yeats's other seekers in the early poetry do not seem to be aware of existing in a state of separation. The key to the problem may lie in this very fact. In the more detailed accounts of the search, *The Wanderings of Oisin* and *The Shadowy Waters,* Oisin and Forgael are in some way involved with an immortal lover. Oisin is led on his unsuccessful journey by Niamh, who is from the immortal world, and Forgael expects to find an immortal lover. Just before he accepts Dectora at the end of the play, he says to her:

> I will have none of you.
> My love shakes out her hair upon the streams
> Where the world ends, or runs from wind to wind
> And eddy to eddy. Masters of our dreams,
> Why have you cloven me with a mortal love?
> Pity these weeping eyes!
> (1900 version, ll. 415–420)

On first consideration, if reality is the fusion of the mortal with the immortal, the mortal hero should seek an immortal lover. This, however, does not seem to be the case. The seekers are heroic, but they are also human; the other half of each must also be human. Together the mortal lovers find an immortal love.

Fragmentation of the self is not an open problem for the early seekers, perhaps because, in the case of Oisin and Forgael, they are not cognizant of it as a problem; or perhaps, in the case of Fergus, it does not exist. It is significant in this connection that Fergus achieves a state of enlightenment without a lover and that Forgael longs for an immortal lover even at the end of the play.

It is significant also that none of the seekers are happy in their present state. In the discussion above, it was noted that we do not learn Fergus's own thoughts in "Who Goes with Fergus?" although we are told that he has become one to follow; but he expresses a definite dissatisfaction even after enlightenment in "Fergus and the Druid." The feelings of all the seekers are similar to those of Mongan in "He thinks of his Past Greatness when a Part of the Constellations of Heaven":

> I have drunk ale from the Country of the Young
> And weep because I know all things now:
> I have been a hazel-tree, and they hung
> The Pilot Star and the Crooked Plough
> Among my leaves in times out of mind:
> I became a rush that horses tread:
> I became a man, a hater of the wind,
> Knowing one, out of all things, alone, that his head
> May not lie on the breast nor his lips on the hair
> Of the woman that he loves, until he dies.
> O beast of the wilderness, bird of the air,
> Must I endure your amorous cries?

The spiritual-physical conflict is very apparent here, and it is also very apparent that this conflict has not been resolved. However, the poem as quoted here represents a later assessment of the situation. The last two lines of this version were first printed in *Later Poems* in 1922. In the earlier printings, including the *Collected Works* of 1908, the last two lines read as follows:

> Although the rushes and the fowl of the air
> Cry of his love with their pitiful cries.

(In the earlier printings, the rest of the poem is substantially the same.) Yeats's stress on the physical emphasizes the split between physical and spiritual much more strongly in the later version. Mongan is torn by the physical love that he can no longer experience. In the earlier version, the creatures show a certain sympathy —even empathy—with Mongan: the fact that the rushes and the fowl pity him in his heavenly existence shows that he has not completely lost contact with them. The sympathy found in the earlier version and the indifference of the later reveal the difference in outlook between the earlier and the later Yeats. In the earlier, there is dissatisfaction and frustration, but there is still an identity with the landscape and the creatures of the world that contains a hope of resolution without resorting to the "artifice of eternity."

The earlier seekers do not "belong" in their initial existence: Fergus is unhappy as king; Oisin is separated from the heroic world that is dead; Forgael has left the world. They reject their roles in life for the essentials of life itself. Rather than allowing themselves to "become" their occupations and find their identities in the lives the materialistic world has forced upon them, they search for the realization of their true being as visionaries—even though their true roles may also bring sadness. The life of the poet-visionary is not easy, and it will not bring peace.

Leonard E. Nathan observes that Yeats's obscurity concerning the supernatural derives not only from his lack of intellectual maturity and terminology but also from his wish to present the supernatural world as he sees it: "essentially ambiguous, mysterious, even sinister from the human point of view." Nathan remarks upon Yeats's belief that the supernatural world is impersonal and cruel "toward the fragmentary, limited beings who attempted to attain unity with it."[59] The important facts here are that the human beings seeking unity are limited and fragmentary and that the supernatural is ambiguous and sinister from the human point of view. The book from which these statements are taken, *The Tragic Drama of William Butler Yeats,* presents as a major Yeatsian theme "the war between natural and supernatural realities."[60] Perhaps a modification of this view would be more accurate. Yeats does see this war, and he very obviously recognizes its existence; however, he seems to feel that the two realities are really one reality, and that the seeker should strive for their reconciliation. The reason the two realities are not clearly seen as one is that the search is not over. We see the search always from the point of view of the seeker who has not yet reached his final goal.

The seekers in Yeats are limited beings who are trying to overcome their limitations. They are fragmented, and they are searching through obscurity. As they overcome their limitations, they begin to resolve their fragmentation. Resolution of fragmentation, however, does not seem to involve loss of individuality.

Even those far along in the search, Mongan and Fergus, retain their essential being even though they have been many things and lived many lives. Even though Fergus has "grown nothing," it is still Fergus speaking.

The seekers, then, do not resolve themselves into one archetype, and Yeats does not present in each seeker one aspect of a larger whole. What he does present are many seekers, all involved in the same search. Resolution of fragmentation and unity will be found at the end of the search. The seekers' yearnings arc seen in "The Secret Rose." In this poem, the Rose, earthly yet mystical, remote and secret, yet by its very nature close to the soil, symbolizes the goal of the search. The seeker, closely personalized by the use of the pronouns *me* and *I*, longs to be enfolded in the Rose along with many other seekers from other ages—the Magi, Conchubar, Cuchulain, Fergus, and other more generalized seekers who

> . . . dwell beyond the stir
> And tumult of defeated dreams; and deep
> Among pale eyelids, heavy with the sleep
> Men have named beauty. . . .
> (ll. 4-7)

In this poem, the seekers are all heroic but still human; they, by human standards, have been successful and unsuccessful; but judged by a heroic standard, they have all found an aesthetic unity in the Rose. In the Rose the dichotomy between the two worlds is resolved. Thus we do not see the sadness of Mongan and Fergus, which comes from that dichotomy. The symbol of resolution, the Rose, is in sight.

THE QUEST IN ARCADIA AND INDIA

Yeats virtually began his career with the figure of the poet-seeker and the theme of the poetic quest. His early Arcadian works, discussed above, contain all the elements of the poetic quest. *The Island of Statues,* in particular, involves the seeker, the journey, and the island—a lake island that is remarkably similar to Innisfree. Even in the artificial setting of Arcadia, the quest is just as dangerous and uncertain as it is in the later poems. And here Yeats establishes his pattern. The seeker moves from a known land to an unknown, a journey that takes him through a forest to the edge of the water, across the water to an island. These topographical elements are all important in the search, and Yeats uses them, either singly or in combination, again and again throughout his poetry. The main characters are important in exactly the same way. Yeats presents us with the poet-seeker (Almintor), the voices that summon him, the woman (Naschina), and the possessor of wisdom (the Enchantress). All these will figure in later poems as Yeats ponders the quest of the poet.

In *The Island of Statues,* the search takes place within an atmosphere of sadness and shadowy evil. When the island is reached and the enchantment is broken, the awakened sleepers are found to be seekers turned to stone, men from the great ages of the quest, who have experience of Aeneas, "the wanderer"; King Arthur, of the Grail quest legends; the god Pan; and the years of Troy, which led to the wanderings of Odysseus. The seekers awaken in sadness to the knowledge that the worlds and heroes they have known are long dead. The failures of their ancient quests can never be countered with the triumph of success, for they cannot begin anew. Yet, by implication, the search becomes universalized, and Almintor is joined with the great seekers of the past.

The Seeker, which is summarized in connection with the possessor of wisdom, adds another complexity to the poetic search. The siren-like voice lures the Knight to his death, but he dies only when he sees the mirror image of himself. The ambiguous figure, the witch who calls him "lover," does not know who she is—it is men who have named her Infamy. Knowledge of self rather than malignant evil seems to be the direct cause of death.

After writing *The Island of Statues* and *The Seeker,* Yeats rejected the Arcadian search almost as soon as it began:

> The woods of Arcady are dead,
> And over is their antique joy;
> Of old the world on dreaming fed;
> Grey truth is now her painted toy;
> Yet still she turns her restless head:
>   (ll. 1-5)

Familiar to most readers of Yeats as "The Song of the Happy
Shepherd" from the *Crossways* volume, this poem (as quoted
above, but with a period rather than a colon after "head" in line
5) was first printed in *The Dublin University Review*, October
1885, as "An Epilogue to 'The Island of Statues' and 'The
Seeker.'" This poem, which evokes a mood of sadness over the
passing of golden days, of the almost bitter feeling that "Words
alone are certain good" (l. 10), that

> The wandering earth herself may be
> Only a sudden flaming word,
> In clanging space a moment heard,
> Troubling the endless reverie
> (ll. 18–21)

is more concerned with the passing of old dreams and old heroes
than with the assertion of line 10 that has provided so many
students and critics with a chapter title. In its next printing, in
The Wanderings of Oisin and Other Poems (1889), the title was
changed to "Song of the Last Arcadian." It was not until its
publication in *Poems* (1895) that it was titled "The Song of the
Happy Shepherd." By 1895, the shepherd could be happy because
Arcady as a poetic setting was dead for Yeats: he knew by then
that Ireland, not the re-creation of an artificial land (which did,
at times, fleetingly resemble County Sligo), was the true location
of his search.

In the meantime, however, having abandoned the possibility
of an artistic Eden in Arcadia, Yeats redirected his search, this
time to a romanticized conception of India. When Yeats leaves
Arcadia and turns to India as a setting, the quest becomes more
remote in feeling. In the Indian poems, Yeats seems to be musing
upon the poetic search; as a result, these poems assume the nature
of meditations upon the quest rather than the recounting of an
actual living search. The lush greenery, exotic names, and remote
time seem even further removed from Europe than the woods
and glades of Arcadia. The Indian poems have about them a
static quality, a serene atmosphere in which the search can be
examined and questioned. Nevertheless, in their evaluation and
consideration of the search, these poems show a deeper concern
and reveal a more sophisticated approach than the Arcadian

works. The search in India develops a maturity that enables
Yeats to consider the search in the more immediate environment
of Ireland. The Indian poems thus serve as a meditative inter-
lude in which Yeats develops and refines the concepts of the
poet-seeker. The Indian poems become, in a real sense, Arcadia
—their setting and mood are pastoral, and their purpose is to give
the poet renewal through quiet meditation.

"Kanva on Himself," published in *The Wanderings of Oisin
and Other Poems,* could well have been spoken by Fergus. Kanva
is enveloped in the sadness of the seeker who has reached the
point of knowing all. He questions his mood and meditates upon
his state of being, using the logic of a "since-then" argument.
Although he has been through many incarnations and has experi-
enced all levels of life, Kanva has "numerous tears" and fears
"the usury of Time" and "Death that cometh with the next life-
key." He has remained within the mortal realm, and he fears
death and time with a mortal fear. He has been unable to attain
a union of mortal with immortal.

The question Why fear time and death, since all forms of life
have been experienced? remains in essence unanswered. Kanva
approaches a resolution at the end of the poem when he achieves
resignation in poetry:

> Then wherefore fear the usury of Time,
> Or Death that cometh with the next life-key?
> Nay, rise and flatter her with golden rhyme,
> For as things were so shall things ever be. . . .
>   (ll. 17-20)

This poem, though outwardly concerning an Indian, expresses
what is really a European version of Oriental resignation to the
cycles of birth and rebirth. Kanva's wisdom does not give him
the contentment of the sage; he has not found peace. Like
Fergus in "Fergus and the Druid," Kanva has known all: he
seems very close to the "great webs of sorrow" of which Fergus
was conscious.

Similarly, but in a more complex fashion, "Anashuya and
Vijaya" is a symbolic meditation on the goal of the search. The
setting gives the symbolic reference:

> *A little Indian temple in the Golden Age. Around it*
> *a garden; around that the forest.*

The setting consists of circles within circles, with the symbolic forest as the circumference. It seems evident that Yeats had in mind the esoteric symbol of the circle and its center, based on the concept that "to leave the circumference for the centre is equivalent to moving from the exterior to the interior, from form to contemplation, from multiplicity to unity, from space to spacelessness, from time to timelessness."[61] Further, Yeats's studies probably told him that

A great many ritual acts have the sole purpose of finding out the spiritual "Centre" of a locality, which then becomes the site, either in itself or by virtue of the temple built upon it, of an "image of the world. . . ."[62]

The similarity of the setting of "Anashuya and Vijaya" to the ritual mentioned above is so striking that one cannot help but feel that Yeats was aware of it. Even though, for the sake of clarity and brevity, the concept of leaving the circumference for the center and the ritual acts involved in this concept were quoted from a modern source, J. E. Circlot's *Dictionary of Symbols,* Yeats's reading in and discussions of esoteric matters made him quite familiar with such matters.

The action of this poetic drama takes place around the center, the place of life, oneness, and unity. However, there is little unity here. Although the atmosphere established at the beginning is one of static peace and tranquillity, yet Anashuya, in her first speech, must pray for peace. There is a contrast throughout the poem between sadness and joy, epitomized by Anashuya's song of the stars:

> A sad, sad thought went by me slowly:
> Sigh, O you little stars! O sigh and shake your blue apparel!
> The sad, sad thought has gone from me now wholly:
> Sing, O you little stars! O sing and raise your rapturous carol
> To mighty Brahma, he who made you many as the sands,
> And laid you on the gates of evening with his quiet hands.
>
> (ll. 17-22)

And the tension of jealousy ("Jealousy" was the original title of the poem) is sustained from beginning to end.

Unity has not brought oneness, tranquillity has not brought peace, and knowledge has not brought happiness. The play is permeated with an atmosphere of wandering, but since the action has reached the center of life, the wandering now becomes aimless. Vijaya is "wandering in the forest," and the sacred flamingoes

> . . . seek their wonted perches
> Within the temple, devious walking, made
> To wander by their melancholy minds.
> (ll. 31–33)

The stars are sad through knowledge, and Beauty, "ever pacing on the verge of things" (l. 53), is a phantom living in a mist of tears. The two lovers may be isolated and alone, but Anashuya's doubt mars their tranquillity and potential oneness. Vijaya unconsciously addresses Anashuya with the name "Amrita," thus giving cause for jealousy, and one line from Anashuya's beginning prayer—"And if he love another, / May panthers end him" —hints at the evil and uneasiness that underlie the action. The tranquillity that should exist in the temple grove in the Golden Age is present on the surface, but underneath there is an undertone of sadness and unrest. The mood is summarized in Vijaya's song:

> Sing you of her, O first few stars
> Whom Brahma, touching with his finger, praises, for you hold
> The van of wandering quiet; ere you be too calm and old,
> Sing, turning in your cars,
> Sing, till you raise your hands and sigh, and from your
>   carheads peer,
> With all your whirling hair, and drop many an azure tear.
> (ll. 41–46)

"The Indian to His Love" is a meditation upon love and the island. Like Innisfree, the island in this poem is a place of dreaming tranquillity:

> The island dreams under the dawn
> And great boughs drop tranquillity. . . .
> (ll. 1-2)

This mood, however, is swiftly broken in the fourth and fifth lines:

> A parrot sways upon a tree,
> Raging at his own image in the enamelled sea.

The outward mood is sustained by the swaying movement and the "enamelled sea," but the parrot himself introduces violent color and emotion. The parrot, like the old knight in *The Seeker,* sees his reflected self. In a subhuman creature, the reflection provokes "raging," not death. When examined in this connection the function of the parrot is two-fold. His very presence adds, by suggestion, vivid color to the island, and he serves to remind the reader of consciousness of being.

The raucous color and noise of the parrot—noise and turbulence are suggested by the use of *raging,* whether it be mental or vocal —is immediately countered by a description of the dreaming idyll the lovers expect to find on the island. In the first version (*Dublin University Review,* December 1886) and *The Wanderings of Oisin,* 1889, the island is a paradise of eternal love:

> There dreamy Time lets fall his sickle
> And Life the sandals of her fleetness,
> And sleek young Joy is no more fickle,
> And Love is kindly and deceitless,
> And Life is over save the murmur and the sweetness.
> (ll. 5a-5e)

In later versions, this stanza was omitted, and the raging of the parrot was followed by the following lines (which, in substance, are in both versions):

> Here we will moor our lonely ship
> And wander ever with woven hands,

> Murmuring softly lip to lip,
> Along the grass, along the sands,
> Murmuring how far away are the unquiet lands. . . .
>
> (ll . 6–10)

The poem ends as follows:

> The heavy boughs, the burnished dove
> That moans and sighs a hundred days:
> How when we die our shades will rove,
> When eve has hushed the feathered ways,
> With vapoury footsole by the water's drowsy blaze.
>
> (ll. 16–20)

Thus, even in the first version, the tranquillity of paradise contains within its very nature the mood of wandering and the consciousness of death. Though not as intense as in "Anashuya and Vijaya," sadness is present.

The Indian poems are meditations on the bittersweet mood found in settings that symbolize tranquillity and static being. The peace of the setting cannot be fully realized by those who inhabit it, whether they be human or animal. A tension is thus created between static peace and restless wandering, indicating an unconscious awareness that the temple and the island, or the state of knowing all forms of life, is not the end of the search. The seeker, possessed by a spirit of restlessness, must still meditate and wander until he reaches the true goal.

After the Indian interlude, the nature of the search is better formulated. Yeats can now move to the more immediate setting of Ireland in the historical and legendary past and in the present. Here the search becomes more intense and more personal. Many of the seekers, like Oisin, have a reality of their own before Yeats uses them in the context of the poetic quest. Thus their legendary heroic personalities become fused with the aspirations of the poet-seeker, and by this fusion the poems in which they appear gain more depth and reality. The search in the Irish poems does not appear to be abstracted from the world in which men live. The artificiality of storybook Arcadia and romanticized India is replaced by the reality of the soil trod by Yeats himself.

CHAPTER FIVE

THE QUEST IN IRELAND

Compared with the Arcadian and Indian poems, the search
in Ireland is more complex and more firmly embedded in reality.
The setting itself is responsible for much of this change. Even
when the time is remote and the geographical setting is unknown
(as in *The Shadowy Waters*), Irish characters and Irish allusions
keep the poems firmly oriented toward the realities of earth. The
supernatural is always seen in relation to the natural: even in
those poems that many critics, such as Dorothy Hoare, Norman
Jeffares, J. Middleton Murry, and R. P. Blackmur, say are vague
and ambiguous, there is some touch of reality, be it only a field-
mouse or the mention of a woman's hair.

The seekers are now more individualized and concrete. Yeats
often adapts to his purpose figures from Irish legend, thereby
enabling the reader to envision the poetic search against the
background of the heroic age and in its relation to the modern
world.

The elements of the search in Arcadia and India are still present:
the journey itself, the forest, the water's edge, the water, the
island, the seeker, the voices that summon him, the woman,
and the possessor of wisdom. These elements, moreover, seem
far less allegorical in their Irish settings. Yeats is exploring the
poetic quest from various aspects and angles, seeking the true
reality that lies behind the apparent opposition of natural and
spiritual.

The heightened complexity and reality can be seen in Yeats's first long Irish poem, *The Wanderings of Oisin*. In this poem, Yeats juxtaposes not only the natural and the spiritual but also the heroic age (represented by Oisin) and the modern world (represented by Saint Patrick). Yeats tells us in a note that the events of the poem "are supposed to have taken place rather in the indefinite period, made up of many periods, described by the folk-tales, than in any particular century." As in the Indian and Arcadian poems, there is still a vagueness, a remoteness, an air of mystery in the setting. However, the remoteness and the use of more than one period do not suggest unreality but, rather, universality. Oisin becomes symbolic of the hero and all that pagan Ireland represents. And Saint Patrick, as the founder of modern Christian Ireland, and with his prosaic dogmatic views, as I have intimated above, becomes the archetype of the modern timid middle-class man. The frames of reference surrounding the names of Oisin and Saint Patrick and the concrete landscape details maintain universality within a setting specific enough to prevent an atmosphere of total vagueness.

The specifics found in the landscapes of Arcadia have become more forceful and direct. Here we see clearly Yeats's use of landscape discussed in Chapter 1. Within the otherwordly atmosphere, the reader is also aware of the reality of the West of Ireland:

> When we followed a deer with our baying hounds,
> With Bran, Sceolan, and Lomair,
> And passing the Firbolgs' burial-mounds,
> Came to the cairn-heaped grassy hill
> Where passionate Maeve is stony-still. . . .
>   (I, 14–18)

The heroic world is a part of the landscape, and Oisin meets Niamh, his lover from the world of faerie, in an exact location in County Sligo that, as we have seen earlier, is very important to Yeats: on the edge of the sea near Knocknarea, on top of which Maeve's cairn still stands. The vagueness of the age of heroes and folk-tales becomes fused with reality; prehistory merges with history and the landscape, which is still physically present. The mystical edge of the sea is now a real seacoast, not some dim Arcadian or Indian shore. The point of departure from the natural to the supernatural is now definitely fixed in the natural world. And Yeats characteristically maintains an underlying tension through the use of striking contrasts: the dead queen, Maeve, "stony-still," is referred to as though she were still alive and full of passion.

In the meeting of natural and supernatural, poetry plays an important part. In the pattern seen in the earlier poems, the hero was usually summoned to his quest by a mysterious voice. In *The Wanderings of Oisin* there is a dual summons. Niamh herself is summoned by poetry to seek Oisin's love:

> "I loved no man, though kings besought,
> Until the Danaan poets brought
> Rhyme that rhymed upon Oisin's name...."
> (I, 62–64)

Niamh is summoned to the wisdom and actions of earth, just as she summons Oisin to the timeless peace of eternity:

> "O Oisin, mount by me and ride
> To shores by the wash of the tremulous tide,
> Where men have heaped no burial-mounds,
> And the days pass by like a wayward tune,
> Where broken faith has never been known,
> And the blushes of first love never have flown...."
> (I, 80–85)

The world to which Niamh calls Oisin, however, is an idealized version of earth, a land of happiness and no sorrow:

> "And there I will give you a hundred hounds;
> No mightier creatures bay at the moon;
> And a hundred robes of murmuring silk,
> And a hundred calves and a hundred sheep
> Whose long wool whiter than sea-froth flows,
> And a hundred spears and a hundred bows,
> And oil and wine and honey and milk,
> And always never-anxious sleep;

> While a hundred youths, mighty of limb,
> But knowing nor tumult nor hate nor strife,
> And a hundred ladies, merry as birds,
> Who when they dance to a fitful measure
> Have a speed like the speed of the salmon herds,
> Shall follow your horn and obey your whim,
> And you shall know the Danaan leisure;
> And Niamh be with you for a wife."
>
> (I, 86-101)

Niamh's experience shows that poetry has the power to link supernatural and natural; this very fact implies that poetry may be the means Yeats is seeking to reveal the true unity of physical and spiritual being.

Even though, on the other hand, the separation between physical and spiritual is constantly emphasized throughout *The Wanderings of Oisin,* Yeats does not present this separation as a "war."[63] He stresses the facts that each world is conscious of the other, that each world is dependent upon the other, and that each world needs the other. Oisin is mortal and Niamh is immortal; yet Niamh feels a strong need for Oisin's love, and Oisin can live in the land of the immortals for three hundred years. In order to die, in fact, his foot must touch the soil of earth, of reality. Presumably, had his foot not touched the earth, he would have had eternal life. Nevertheless, Oisin can never lose the "mortal sadness of earth"; his nature cannot change. The tone of the poem suggests that Oisin could never be content in the land of the immortals any more than he could in the grey Christian world of Saint Patrick.

As we have seen in the preceding chapter, the mortal world can never lose sight of earth. When the immortals sing of their joy, their happiness is seen in contrast to the sadness of the world of mortal men. In essence, the land of the immortals is lonely; its joy is permeated with a tone of sadness:

> "But we in a lonely land abide
> Unchainable as the dim tide,
> With hearts that know nor law nor rule,
> And hands that hold no wearisome tool,
> Folded in love that fears no morrow,
> Nor the grey wandering osprey sorrow."
>
> (I, 337-342)

The first version contains nine additional lines that make the point more obvious. The earlier passage reads as follows:

> "But we, oh rolling stars, are free.
> The ever-winding wakeful sea,
> That hides us from all human spying,
> Is not so free, so free, so free.
> Our hands have known no wearying tool,
> Our lives have known no law nor rule;
> Afar from where the years are flying
> O'er men who sleep, and wake, and die,
> And peak and pine we know not why,
> We only know that we were glad
> Aforetime, and shall not grow sad
> Or tired on any dawning morrow,
> Nor ever change or feel the clutches
> Of grievous Time on his old crutches,
> Or fear the wild grey osprey sorrow."

In the earlier version, the immortal land is not said to be lonely, but it is definitely isolated, cut off by the sea from the lands of men. The freedom and happiness of the immortals is again seen through contrast with men and even the sea. Yet the detailed description of the sadness of men and, in both versions, the repeated mention of the "grey osprey sorrow" lend a feeling of mournfulness that belies the expression of joy by those who are freer than the sea. The isolation of the immortal world is not total: it is dependent on the other world for images, activities, and ideas.

The interdependency of the natural and spiritual worlds in *The Wanderings of Oisin* exemplifies Yeats's theory of metaphor and symbol as described by Parkinson. Parkinson, following Yeats's ideas in "The Necessity of Symbolism," observes that Yeats believes in two worlds, the natural and the spiritual, but that these worlds differ in value, not in substance. Thus objects and symbols from the natural world may be used to invoke the spiritual and eternal world.[64] Thus in Yeats's poetry, especially in the early poetry that does not depend upon *A Vision,* we are not dealing with what William James calls a "closed system." Yeats is searching for the true reality that exists behind the apparent cleavage between what we see as natural and spiritual.

The problem of true reality is central in *The Wanderings of Oisin*. The "real" world at the time of the dialogue between Oisin and Saint Patrick is the modern world that Saint Patrick has introduced. Yet, even though the modern world has supplanted the world of the pagan heroes, the heroic world still exists in the person and in the mind of Oisin: at the end of the poem, Oisin is able to reject the world of Saint Patrick in order to "dwell in the house of the Fenians, be they in flames or at feast" (III, 224). Also, the existence of the Christian world does not cancel out the equally real existence of the pagan Tir-na-n-og, wherein Oisin wandered for three hundred years. The problem of reality in this poem becomes an ambiguous one that is never solved. The mortal and immortal, Oisin and Niamh, need each other; yet by their very natures they can never be joined.

The ambiguity here should not be termed conscious, since it is unavoidable. Yeats is recounting an unsuccessful but heroic quest, one that raises questions that are, for the time being at least, unanswerable. The most important of these questions concerns the possibility of the search in the modern world. In the world represented by Saint Patrick, Oisin is a pagan in need of conversion and Niamh is an evil demon. The age of heroes is dead: on Oisin's return to Ireland after three hundred years of wandering, an old man tells him, " 'The Fenians a long time are dead' " (III, 172). Men no longer have the strength of heroes. Oisin sees two men staggering and falling under their burden. The world he returns to is weak and grey; men lack the courage, strength, and imagination necessary to engage in an adventure of any sort. The heroic virtues must be regained before men can attain the poetic vision. Even Oisin was held back by his mortal nature, and after he had seen the modern world, he lost the vision of his search:

> And the dreams of the islands were gone, and I knew
> how men sorrow and pass,
> And their hound, and their horse, and their love,
> and their eyes that glimmer like silk.
>   (III, 175–176)

Yet, in spite of all, Oisin remains heroic until the end. Saint

Patrick's victory is not complete. Physically, Oisin has been conquered by the world and time; spiritually, he remains victorious. Nevertheless, Saint Patrick has conquered to the extent that the men now living in Ireland consider the heroic pagan world to be a part of the dead past that holds no meaning for them. Faced with the difficult task of being a poet in the world of Saint Patrick, Yeats attempted to revive the virtues of the heroic world, not just for other men but for himself as well. As Zwerdling observes, "For Yeats, the most appealing quality of this world was its emphasis on the power of the solitary individual, its concentration on the uniqueness possible in a society, unlike that of the modern city, in which people, events, and institutions are recognized as unique."[65] We see in *The Wanderings of Oisin* a part of Yeats's own search. Yeats, like Oisin, is hampered by the "fluttering sadness of earth"; and, like Oisin and Niamh, Yeats does not know where to find the Isle of Youth. For Yeats the heroic world of the epic tales is anything but imaginary. It contains a reality that the modern world has lost and needs desperately. According to his theory of symbolism, Yeats felt that he could use characters, events, topography, and pure symbols in such a way that he could awaken in himself and others those values that are apparently forgotten and lost but are still alive in the Great Memory of the race.

Yeats relies on the power of evocation to awaken in the reader the archetypal truths, but his symbols do not operate in a system of one-to-one ratios. It is for this reason that Morton Seiden's interpretation of *The Wanderings of Oisin,* although interesting, is not very useful. Seiden reaches the conclusion that Yeats has so modified his source (a translation from the Gaelic of an eighteenth-century poem, "The Lay of Oisin in the Land of Youth" by Michael Comyn) that *The Wanderings of Oisin* "seems to be mainly a synthesis of Theosophical dogma, of Rhys' *The Hibbert Lectures,* and of William Morris' *The Earthly Paradise,* Shelley's *Prometheus Unbound,* and Blake's *The Four Zoas.*"[66] Seiden then quotes from Yeats's letter to Katherine Tynan in which he says that *Oisin* is an arrangement of private symbols, to which only he has the key. Seiden feels, however, that by studying the poem against the poet's life and *A Vision,* he has interpreted the symbolism:

I take the four islands to be the cosmic quaternaries; the opposition of
Tirnanog and Ireland, the cosmic antinomies; and Oisin's journey into and
out of Tirnanog, the cyclical movement of human life. "The Wanderings of
Oisin" thus foreshadows, if implicitly, not only much of *A Vision* but also,
though composed at the outset of his career, the mythological patterns of
Yeats's later poetry.[67]

If the source—or sources—have been modified to this extent,
then it is far more important to see what Yeats produced than
to delve into the poem in an attempt—almost guaranteed to be
somewhat futile—to find the sources that underlie his treatment
of the wanderer theme. In fact, Yeats states in a note dated 1912
that "the poem is founded upon the Middle Irish dialogues of
Saint Patrick and Oisin and a certain Gaelic poem of the last
century." He goes on to say that "the Gaelic poems do not
make Oisin go to more than one island, but a story in *Silva
Gadelica* describes 'four paradises,' an island to the north, an
island to the west, an island to the south, and Adam's paradise in
the east."[68] The specific source, then, can be analyzed as a
composite that has been greatly altered to fit Yeats's own individ-
ual purposes.

The symbolism, too, is hidden from the reader, probably be-
cause Yeats wants to avoid exact and mechanical interpretations
such as that proposed by Mr. Seiden. Yeats wants to evoke in the
reader a consciousness of the ancient and universal theme of the
journey that is found in the *Odyssey,* the *Aeneid,* the *Divine
Comedy,* to mention three of the most famous literary treat-
ments of the theme. The archetypal nature of the journey is
seen in its almost universal appearance in various times and
places; in Yeats's own tradition it appears in pagan form in the
folk-tales called *echtrae* (adventures) and *immrama* (voyages),
and in Christian versions of these same folk-tale types, such as
the *Voyage of Saint Brendan.*[69] In Yeats's own time and in the
literature of nineteenth-century England there are many treat-
ments: in Wordsworth, in Shelley, and, as Seiden mentions, in
William Morris (it appears in *The Well at the World's End* as
well as in *The Earthly Paradise*).

These adventures and voyages, and specifically the ancient
Irish *echtrae* and *immrama,* have a common focus in accounts
of journeys to the Promised Land or to the Other World.[70]

William Morris's consciously archaic Argument to *The Earthly Paradise* can serve as a summary of this common concern:

Certain gentlemen and mariners of Norway, having considered all that they had heard of the Earthly Paradise, set sail to find it, and after many troubles and the lapse of many years came old men to some western land, of which they had never before heard: there they died, when they had dwelt there certain years, much honoured of the strange people.[71]

The ending has many variations. Quite often the seeker will return, like Saint Brendan, a holy man. However, the fact that many general parallels can be drawn between *The Wanderings of Oisin* and these other stories, ancient and modern, is far more significant than any specific parallel or variation, of which there are many. Yeats definitely wants the reader to be aware of the antiquity and universality of the search. Very likely it is for this reason that he said to Katherine Tynan in the letter mentioned above that "the romance is for my readers."

As the foregoing discussion shows, in *The Wanderings of Oisin* Yeats, for the most part, follows the search pattern found in the Arcadian and Indian poems, though here the pattern is far more complex. To summarize, the mortal seeker, Oisin, and the immortal seeker, Niamh, are both summoned to the quest: Niamh by poetry and Oisin, in turn, by Niamh herself. The "voice" has become more directly involved and is indeed a part of the seekers. They travel on horseback from the edge of the sea to three islands in search of heroic contentment. So far, with the exception of the forest, which is present but not directly connected with the search, the pattern is maintained: the summoning voice, the woman, the water's edge, the journey over water, and the island. In this poem, however, there is an interesting variation in the search pattern: there is no true possessor of wisdom. The antiheroic nature of Saint Patrick prevents him from seeing anything other than a grey Christian universe antagonistic to the heroic ideal and all that it represents. Potentially, Saint Patrick could be a link between physical and spiritual. He is a man of great wisdom and great spiritual power. He has fought battles on the mortal and the immortal level in order to conquer and convert Ireland. Nevertheless, his beliefs, his office, and his very nature prevent him from realizing this potential on

a universal scale. He is frozen in a Christian context, and he
stands between the Christian universe and the pagan, in the at-
titude of eternal opposition seen in his dialogue with Oisin:

> *S. Patrick.*   Be still: the skies
> Are choked with thunder, lightning, and fierce wind,
> For God has heard, and speaks His angry mind;
> Go cast your body on the stones and pray,
> For He has wrought midnight and dawn and day.
>
> *Oisin.* Saint, do you weep? I hear amid the thunder
> The Fenian horses; armour torn asunder;
> Laughter and cries. The armies clash and shock,
> And now the daylight-darkening ravens flock.
> Cease, cease, O mournful, laughing Fenian horn!
>   (II, 204–213)

The "Song of Monks" from the first version makes the Christian
position all too clear:

> "Each one a horsehair shirt hath on,
> And many *Pater nosters* said since dawn.
> Trembling, on the flags we fall,
> Fearful of the thunder-ball,
> Yet do with us whate'er thou wilt,
> For great our error, great our guilt."
>   (II, 208c–h)

These lines were placed between Saint Patrick's admonition
and Oisin's reply. In contrast to this cringing world, Oisin asserts
the heroic ideal; he and Niamh are forced to rely on themselves
and on each other, and on the Danaan poets who summoned
Niamh to seek Oisin's love. They seek to the limits of their own
knowledge and ability; beyond that, they are doomed to failure.
Nevertheless, even when conquered by time and mortality, Oisin
does not surrender. And Niamh, left behind in the land of the
Immortals, presumably still mourns for him.

At the end of his wanderings, the pattern of Oisin's journey is
inverted. The world of the Immortals is now as grey as the new
Ireland, and Oisin's return echoes the beginning of the search—
through the forest to the sea's edge and across the water.

Oisin rejects the Immortals for the heroes, but the poem has not come full circle, since the world of the heroes no longer exists. When he cannot find true union of mortal and immortal, the supernatural world seems lifeless. The horse comes to him knowing that he wants to "leave the Immortals, their dimness, their dews dropping sleep" (III, 108). Oisin's spiritual condition is beautifully described with the pathetic metaphor of the forsaken galley:

> "Like me were some galley forsaken far off in Meridian
> isle,
> Remembering its long-oared companions, sails turning to
> threadbare rags;
> No more to crawl on the seas with long oars mile after
> mile,
> But to be amid shooting of flies and flowering of
> rushes and flags."
>
> (III, 117-120)

Perfect unity involves a true fusion of the physical with the spiritual. Almost ironically, the "strange horse" who knows Oisin's longings and carries him back to earth seems to come closer to a union of natural and supernatural being than either Oisin or Niamh. This mysterious creature, however, cannot return Oisin to the world for which he longs. Oisin wants the poem to come full circle: he does not wish solely to return to the mortal world; he yearns for the heroic world that he left three hundred years before. When he finds the world changed, he rejects the new world that has replaced the land of the Fenians just as vehemently as he spurned the dim world of the Immortals. Oisin is still engaged in the same search—he is looking for the Isle of Youth where the heroic world of Ireland can live forever. An immortal heroic world is not to be found either on the three islands of Tir-na-n-og or in the land of Saint Patrick.

In *The Wanderings of Oisin,* then, the seeker is a tragic hero, affirming his existence and that of his companions of the heroic age, opposing himself against the existence of the conquering grey world of Saint Patrick. The poem is a positive statement affirming the heroic man—whom Yeats later called the subjective man—and a lament over the objective world that does not recognize the existence of the heroic virtues.

The positive nature and the vigor of *The Wanderings of Oisin* are more than obvious when it is compared with Swinburne's "Hymn to Proserpine," published eleven years earlier. The situation in both poems is very similar; the tone of both poems is dreamlike; the mood is even enhanced by similar verse forms, especially when Book III of *Oisin* is compared with "Proserpine." Within the twilight world of both poems, the pagan ends in old age and death. From this point, however, the differences are more important than the similarities. In Swinburne, the attitude is one of resigned acceptance:

> So long as I endure, no longer; and laugh not again,
>   neither weep.
> For there is no God found stronger than death; and
>   death is a sleep.
>
> (ll. 109–110)

In Yeats, on the other hand, Oisin ends courageously, even though in the Christian world, reaffirming to Saint Patrick the old heroic spirit:

> It were sad to gaze on the blessèd and no man I loved
>   of old there;
> I throw down the chain of small stones! when life in
>   my body has ceased,
> I will go to Caoilte, and Conan, and Bran, Sceolan,
>   Lomair,
> And dwell in the house of the Fenians, be they in
>   flames or feast.
>
> (III, 221–224)

Although Swinburne, like Yeats, implies a cyclical universe in which the Christian God will one day be replaced by another ("Yet thy kingdom shall pass, Galilean, thy dead shall go down to thee dead"), the "Hymn to Proserpine" has an air of finality about it. In Yeats the conclusion is not final. Although the touch of earth returns Oisin to mortality, it does not send him to the oblivion of nonbeing nor to the stillness of sleep. Niamh's world continues to exist; the possibility of another search, even one beginning in the antiheroic modern world, has not been removed.

Niamh and Oisin may not be able to find the Island of Content or Youth, and none may know where it is; yet its existence is not denied.

Unlike the accepted Pre-Raphaelite stereotype of vague, languid mistiness, the Celtic Twilight seen in *The Wanderings of Oisin* is vital. Swinburne's dimness implies death; Yeats's affirms life. Yeats's twilight is a vague dimness only to those who cannot see through and beyond it. It represents the true reality beyond the outward world of appearances: the world of the dream, or in one sense, a return to Eden. It is the reality Yeats presents in "Into the Twilight," already quoted above, in which he urges: "Come clear of the nets of wrong and right."

In "Into the Twilight" and "To Some I have Talked with by the Fire," Yeats contrasts the restricted world of Saint Patrick— represented by the "wrong and right" of middle-class Christianity —with the freedom of the twilight world, in which the dream and the vision are not categorized. In "To Some I have Talked with by the Fire," Yeats speaks of

> . . . the wayward twilight companies
> Who sigh with mingled sorrow and content,
> Because their blossoming dreams have never bent
> Under the fruit of evil and of good. . . .
> (ll. 6-9)

It should be noted that the sighing here is not from languor but from sorrow. The Yeatsian Eden is not a place of sterile content-ment: emotions are essential to the passionate life; bliss and sadness must both be experienced. It is also important that the "wayward twilight companies" sigh *because* their dreams are not weighted down by the good and evil of Saint Patrick. And further, the dreams are "blossoming," in contrast to the dead imaginations of the men Oisin finds in the Ireland dominated by the Church.

From this standpoint, the aesthetic concern of Yeats's poetry, and the poetic quest, can be seen in a religious perspective. The poems are religious in the sense that all great poetry is religious, but no more than that. Yeats states in the *Autobiographies:*

I had, when we first made our Society [the Hermetic Society of the Golden Dawn], proposed for our consideration that whatever the great poets had affirmed in their finest moments was the nearest we could come to an authoritative religion, and that their mythology, their spirits of water and wind, were but literal truth. I had read *Prometheus Unbound* with this thought in mind and wanted help to carry my study through all literature.[72]

This statement should not, however, be taken alone. Yeats later observed that

if Shelley had nailed his Prometheus, or some equal symbol, upon some Welsh or Scottish rock, . . . [his] art would have entered more intimately, more microscopically, as it were, into our thought and given perhaps to modern poetry a breadth and stability like that of ancient poetry.[73]

Within a native context, then, the power of evocation would be stronger, because less artificial, and the poet could better evoke in the reader images that "well up before the mind's eye from a deeper source than conscious or subconscious memory."[74]

Thus "Eden" is evocative rather than literal. Yeats's use of "wrong and right," "good and evil," and Eden are to remind the reader of the first chapter of Genesis and of the theological problems raised by that chapter, but he does not want his readers to dwell solely and specifically upon Biblical matters. He puts these matters in a context of pagan Ireland, and within this framework the reader should see Eden to be of a more general significance, as important to Homer or Yeats as it is to Moses or John Milton. In the introductory lines to *The Shadowy Waters*, sometimes titled "I walked among the Seven Woods of Coole," the significance of Eden is made quite clear:

> How shall I name you, immortal, mild, proud shadows?
> I only know that all we know comes from you,
> And that you come from Eden on flying feet.
> Is Eden far away, or do you hide
> From human thought, as hares and mice and coneys
> That run before the reaping-hook and lie
> In the last ridge of the barley? Do our woods
> And winds and ponds cover more quiet woods,
> More shining winds, more star-glimmering ponds?
> Is Eden out of time and out of space?

> And do you gather about us when pale light
> Shining on water and fallen among leaves,
> And winds blowing from flowers, and whirr of feathers
> And the green quiet, have uplifted the heart?
>
> (ll. 27-40)

In these lines Yeats evokes Eden within the context suggested by his choice of adjectives—"immortal, mild, proud"— and the homely simile of the small animals fleeing and hiding before the reaping hook. This simile and the earthly woods, winds, ponds, and flowers serve to keep the reader within the confines of Coole Park and prevent him from wandering in the exotic delights of a tropical Eden. The Eden here is clearly not the one usually imaged for Adam and Eve, though the prelapsarian state of innocence and immortality contributes to the total image. Eden is the other world, the "deeper source than conscious or subconscious memory," the true reality beyond the world of appearances: the fourth island that Niamh and Oisin could not find.

The metaphorical significance seen in Yeats's use of Eden can also be found in other aspects of his early poetry. In the same way that Eden perhaps exists behind the facade of the present world, the remembrances of the heroic world in *The Wanderings of Oisin,* for example, are more than a nostalgia for past glories: Oisin and others like him did once exist—and perhaps still exist, if we can only penetrate the veil that hides them from the modern world.

Oisin and the other seekers are individuals, with their own historical or legendary histories; but their past lives do not restrict their larger significance in Yeats's poetry. *The Wanderings of Oisin,* as has been demonstrated, is not a simple retelling of the old story, though Yeats retains many elements of the original, such as the hornless deer chased by the phantom hound that is white save for one red ear (I, 139–141). Oisin's stature as an ancient hero gives additional meaning to his role as poet-seeker, and the old story provides Yeats with a framework in which to write. And yet, as Norman Jeffares observes concerning some of Yeats's early poems, "It is not necessary to know the sources of these poems to enjoy them; they are comprehensible and universal in appeal."[75]

No matter what the reader's background may be, these poems always convey meaning because of their use of universal symbols; and because Yeats always controls the general with the particular, the meaning never becomes excessively vague. Even in the poems concerned with the Rose, in which the poetic search receives its most etherealized treatment, Yeats is very careful not to become too vague or abstract. He has many precedents for using the Rose as a symbol of completion or perfection, and her certainly had this connotation in mind, but at the same time he is careful to adhere to the meaning that he later outlines in a note:

> The Rose was part of my second book, The Countess Kathleen and Various Legends and Lyrics, 1892, and I notice upon reading these poems for the first time for several years that the quality symbolised as The Rose differs from the Intellectual Beauty of Shelley and of Spenser in that I have imagined it as suffering with man and not as something pursued and seen from afar.[76]

The Rose is not specifically defined as Intellectual Beauty, the Rose of Rosicrucianism, or Ireland, to name three possible meanings. Yeats does not restrict himself to the point that he comes close to allegory. The Rose is ideal and mystic, yet it suffers with man. Its connotations are many, and its only restriction is its relationship with the world. The Rose is united with man through suffering. Again Yeats consistently maintains a specific earthly concern along with the spiritual. Like Yeats's Eden, the Rose is not artificial or totally of the other world. Similar to the concept of the resurrection of the body as found in the New Testament, the Rose is a perfect combination of the eternal and the mortal:

> Rose of all Roses, Rose of all the World!
> You, too, have come where the dim tides are hurled
> Upon the wharves of sorrow, and heard ring
> The bell that calls us on; the sweet far thing.
> Beauty grown sad with its eternity
> Made you of us, and of the dim grey sea.
> ("The Rose of Battle," ll. 25-30)

The Rose is simultaneously in the world and above the world.

It experiences the sorrows of man and lives with man, yet it is also an instrument for a Rosicrucian or Blakean spiritual reconciliation. In "The Rose of Peace," Yeats addresses the Rose directly and develops the following situation: If Saint Michael would look upon the Rose, he would forget his deeds and cease brooding upon the wars of God; mankind, seeing him bow to the Rose, would come to God in peace and love:

> And God would bid His warfare cease,
> Saying all things were well;
> And softly make a rosy peace,
> A peace of Heaven with Hell.
>   (ll. 13-16)

The Rose, in this poem, represents the mystic power of love. As such, it is an active and all-powerful force. The Rose, however, is more than a force or power. It is a tangible, visible object whose symbolism is not limited.

In the initial poem in *The Rose,* "To the Rose upon the Rood of Time," the Rose becomes all things to the poet. It is the inspiration, the voice that summons him; it is the possessor of wisdom; it is a power to be invoked; and it is a spiritual entity that links the poet with his fellow man:

> Come near, that no more blinded by man's fate,
> I find under the boughs of love and hate,
> In all poor foolish things that live a day,
> Eternal beauty wandering on her way.
>
> Come near, come near, come near—Ah, leave me still
> A little space for the rose-breath to fill!
> Lest I no more hear common things that crave;
> The weak worm hiding down in its small cave,
> The field-mouse running by me in the grass,
> And heavy mortal hopes that toil and pass;
> But seek alone to hear the strange things said
> By God to the bright hearts of those long dead,
> And learn to chaunt a tongue men do not know. . . .
>   (ll. 9-21)

The thoughts expressed here are very similar to those of the
Earth in Act IV of Shelley's *Prometheus Unbound:*

> Leave Man, who was a many-sided mirror
> Which could distort to many a shape of error
> This true fair world of things, a sea reflecting love;
> Which over all his kind, as the sun's heaven
> Gliding o'er ocean, smooth, serene, and even,
> Darting from starry depths radiance and life doth move;
> . . . .
> Man, one harmonious soul of many a soul,
> Whose nature is its own divine control,
> Where all things flow to all, as rivers to the sea;
> Familiar acts are beautiful through love;
> Labour, and pain, and grief, in life's green grove
> Sport like tame beasts,—none knew how gentle they could be!
>   (ll. 382-387, 400-405)

In both, the errors of humanity are rejected and the values of
man are asserted; the power of love (in Yeats, the Rose upon
the Cross) is the means of achieving true balance and perspective.
The Rose for Yeats thus becomes a symbol of Unity of Being,
of the reconciliation and union of natural and spiritual for which
the poet is striving. The Rose appears in Yeats's poetry as some-
thing from a dream-vision in which the poet sees beyond himself,
catching a brief glimpse of true reality.

The appearance of the Rose indicates that the poetic search
need not end in frustration and despair. The seekers examined
so far have lacked the vision of the Rose and have therefore
fallen short of their goal. Even Yeats himself, in "The Secret
Rose," invokes it as "Far-off, most secret, and inviolate Rose"
(l. 1), and is awaiting its guidance from afar. Although Yeats is
still searching, the vision of the Rose can be seen as a turning
point in his visionary experience. For the first time he can see a
symbol of unity or reconciliation; unlike Almintor and Oisin,
he can see beyond the island and all it represents, and know that
beyond Innisfree lies hope rather than frustration.

CHAPTER SIX

THE VISION AND THE QUEST

The difficulty of vision concerned Yeats throughout the course of his development. In the Rose poems he sees with greater clarity and his vision is less clouded. There were, however, other aspects of the search that needed examination before he could see the Rose, and the Rose itself is not the end of his search. Unlike Elias, Yeats was not swept up to eternal beatitude in a fiery chariot. There is much to be overcome before pure vision can be attained. In *Prometheus Unbound,* Shelley expresses the idea that man has destroyed his relationship with God and with nature, an idea that is very close to Yeats's opinions about the evils and falseness of modern civilization. If we put Shelley's statement into Yeats's terms, man has created the world of evil and good, the world that Oisin finds after his three hundred years of wandering. To return briefly to some of Yeats's earliest work, the Figure in *The Seeker* says: "Men call me Infamy/ I know not what I am." She is named, defined, and classified by man, not by herself. She is hidden in the forest; man seeks her and finds her. Man can name her, but she is not conscious or sure of her own identity. Even in Byzantium, Unity of Being was not universal—and it is the poets who have gone wrong:

I think that in early Byzantium, maybe never before or since in recorded history, religious, aesthetic and practical life were one, that architect and artificers—though not, it may be, poets, for language had been the instrument of controversy and must have grown abstract—spoke to the multitude and the few alike. The painter, the mosaic worker, the worker in gold and silver, the illuminator of sacred books, were almost impersonal, almost perhaps without the consciousness of individual design, absorbed in their subject-matter and that the vision of a whole people.[77]

Man's corruption, his artificiality and his sophisticated abstractions, have so limited his vision that the process of attaining unity and wisdom is very arduous—so difficult, in fact, that the veil of obscurity is found in the physical world, as with Oisin, and in the immortal world, as with Niamh. Oisin and Niamh, too, are exceptional beings for even attempting the search. Most people are so shrouded by the veil that they see nothing but the world around them, and feel no need for seeing farther.

Two years before the publication of *The Wanderings of Oisin*, Yeats published two poems that have bearing upon the quest and the problem of vision: "The Fairy Pedant" and "The Madness of King Goll." The first shows the search in the land of faerie, and, when considered along with the disillusion and frustration of Oisin and Niamh, negates any idea of fairyland as a land of escape or as the end of a Pre-Raphaelite quest. The second shows a wandering king who, unlike Fergus, is incapable of vision and is driven mad by his experiences.

"The Fairy Pedant," first published in *The Irish Monthly* in 1887 and later reprinted in *The Wanderings of Oisin and Other Poems*, clearly shows that Yeats's Eden, Unity of Being, or true reality is not to be found in the land of faerie. According to the *Irish Monthly* version, the scene is "a circle of Druidic stones" with "a band of fairies following another who goes whispering to herself." The solitary fairy (the phrase used as a title by Yeats in a 1901 version of this poem), wandering in a place suggestive of Druid wisdom, is rebuked by the other fairies in the same way that the solitary wanderers of earth are condemned by their fellow men for trying to escape that which is commonly called "reality":

> Afar from our lawn and our levée,
> O sister of sorrowful gaze!
> Where the roses in scarlet are heavy
> And dream of the end of their days,

> You move in another dominion
> And hang o'er the historied stone:
> Unpruned is your beautiful pinion
> Who wander and whisper alone.
> (ll. 1-8)

The Swinburnian echoes ("O sister of sorrowful gaze!"), the rhythm, and the alliteration serve to place this poem within the Celtic Twilight; the tone, the actions, and the statement of the poem reveal the world of faerie as a counterpart of the world of men.

The fairy's search conforms to the same pattern as that of Oisin or of Niamh. As a baby she heard the summons:

> My mother drew forth from the long grass
> A piece of a nightingale's egg,
> And cradled me here where are sung,
> Of birds even, longings for aery
> Wild wisdoms of spirit and tongue.
> (ll. 23-27)

In spite of the repeated plea of the other fairies that she is "wasting away," the solitary one wishes to remain in the place of Druidic wisdom and in the mortal world, and she entreats the others:

> Ah! cruel ones, leave me alone now
> While I murmur a little and ponder
> The history here in the stone now;
> Then away and away will I wander,
> And measure the minds of the flowers,
> And gaze on the meadow-mice wary,
> And number their days and their hours. . . .
> (ll. 13-19)

The fairy's concern with the Druidic mysteries, the minutiae of the natural world, and her sense of purpose type her as another wanderer like those seen in Arcadia, India, and Ireland. In general terms her search is the same: a wandering from her own world to another. Yet, importantly, she leaves the immortal world for the world of man in her search for wisdom.

"The Fairy Pedant," however, does not present a total reversal
of the direction of the search. The fairy is said to be in "another
dominion" (l. 5). The circle of stones, of course, is on the phys-
ical earth, but twice (ll. 6 and 15) the history of the stones—
their connection with the ancient Druids—is emphasized. The
fairy moves within a circle—a type of island—and is concerned
with the flowers, the meadow-mice, days and hours, and the
history of the stones. The phrase "another dominion" seems to
refer not specifically to the mortal world, but to a spiritual state
that differs from the world of faerie. Taken together with the
fairy's movements within the circle of stones, the other dominion
becomes the same mystical island visited by the other seekers,
the same symbolic fusion of reality and vision. The fairy, in
fact, is trying to go beyond even the world of her own kind, and,
as a solitary, she continues her search for wisdom while the
others, who have not the vision and the hope, turn away, leaving
her—in their minds—to waste away into nothingness.

The poems ends with the repetition of the "come away" re-
frain. She is summoned back to the world of faerie in the same
way that the child is summoned in "The Stolen Child"; yet she
does not wish to leave the circle, the place where she and even
the birds long for "wild wisdoms."

In contrast to the type of search seen so far, in which a hero
or an immortal enters upon a wandering quest for which some
purpose, though unknown, is felt to exist, "The Madness of King
Goll" describes a demented search that begins and ends in mad-
ness and total frustration. King Goll is a wanderer whose vision
becomes distorted and whose call to wisdom is the call to insanity.
"The Madness of King Goll" expresses total disillusion, for the
king's dementia is not the insane ecstasy of true vision, but the
madness of a man swept up in and overwhelmed by the tide of
life.

In the first stanza of the poem, King Goll, like Fergus, is a
powerful king; he is also a man of vision whose powers are like
those of the ancient poets who had control of men and the
elements. He is even recognized as such by the poets or Druids.
His word "drove tumult and war away" (l. 5).

> And every ancient Ollave said,
> While he bent down his fading head,
> "He drives away the Northern cold."
> (ll. 9-11)[78]

Unlike Fergus, King Goll did not seek out the "dreaming wisdom" of the Druids. He is not dissatisfied with the state of kingship; in fact, he possesses much of the wisdom sought by Fergus. As he looks back on his early life, King Goll sees tranquillity and peace. His present emotions—those of madness—are reflected in the foreboding refrain: *"They will not hush, the leaves a-flutter round me, the beech leaves old."*
The change in King Goll takes place after he goes to war, after the transition from tranquillity to conflict. He is infected with a battle fever:

> But slowly, as I shouting slew
> And trampled in the bubbling mire,
> In my most secret spirit grew
> A whirling and a wandering fire. . . .
> (ll. 25-28)

From this point on, the poem becomes a cynical parody of the search. After the call, King Goll proceeds into the woods, as other seekers have done, but his wandering is aimless and erratic. His visionary powers remain, but they are now the powers of madness. In a note in the 1895 edition of *Poems,* Yeats says:

In the legend King Goll hid himself in a valley near Cork, where it is said all the madmen in Ireland would gather were they free, so mighty a spell did he cast over that valley.

Yeats clearly had this legend in mind when he wrote the poem, for King Goll does cast a spell of sorts over the animals:

> I wander on, and wave my hands,
> And sing, and shake my heavy locks.
> The grey wolf knows me; by one ear
> I lead along the woodland deer;
> The hares run by me growing bold.
> (ll. 43-47)

In the immediate context of the poem, however, King Goll is more a part of the animal world than a power over the valley, in direct contrast to his power over men before his madness.

Like Forgael in *The Shadowy Waters,* King Goll acquires a harp (in later versions, a tympan—a Celtic stringed instrument) that has a magical power. Forgael's harp, though, came from Aengus, while King Goll found his "deserted on a doorway seat" (1. 56). For a time, the harp frees King Goll from his madness, but eventually the strings are broken and all hope is lost:

> And as I sang my soul was free
> Of fever. Now the strings are torn
> And I must wail beside the sea
> Or pace and weep in woods forlorn,
> For my remembering hour is done;
> Or fling my laughter to the sun,
> In all his evening vapours rolled. . . .
>> (ll. 65–71 as printed in the first version,
>> *The Leisure Hour,* September 1887)

The later versions, though tighter and more concise, are substantially the same in meaning. King Goll is left in madness in the geographical environment of the search—the edge of the sea or in the woods. His is the most bitter and total defeat suffered by any of the seekers.

Similar feelings of despair and frustration are expressed in a more personal way in "The Everlasting Voices," first published in 1896. Here Yeats does not say that the search is without a purpose, but he does reveal a Mosaic reluctance to be called and to do the work:

> O sweet everlasting Voices, be still;
> Go to the guards of the heavenly fold
> And bid them wander obeying your will. . . .
>> (ll. 1–3)

When the Voices are asked to "Go to the guards of the heavenly fold," the world is seen to be old, incapable, and unworthy: "Have you not heard that our hearts are old . . . ?" (1. 5). The world can no longer produce a spiritual leader. The biblical comparison is striking. Jahweh said to Moses: " 'Come, I will send you to Pharaoh that you may bring forth my people, the sons of Israel, out of Egypt.' But Moses said to God, 'Who am I that I should go to Pharaoh, and bring the sons of Israel out of Egypt?'" (RSV. Exod. 3:10–11). This is not the complaining, the "woe is me," of Jeremiah; it is a statement of *Domine, non sum dignus,* and of the futility of the effort: the task should be given to someone greater.

If the biblical comparisons seem irrelevant, "The Everlasting Voices" should be examined in the light of the poetic quest and of Yeats's theories about the poet and the work of the poet. The seekers were summoned to the search by voices in the same way that the Old Testament prophets were called by God to dedicate themselves to the task of disseminating and proclaiming the inspired word that came to them from God. They were the spokesmen of the divine order and, it was hoped, the instruments of reform. Yeats, in turn, as we have seen, felt that the great poets were also inspired and that the only true religion could be made from the greatest statements of the greatest poets. He too felt that national reform could be brought about by poetry and drama, and he too felt the power of the inspired poetic word:

> Did that play of mine send out
> Certain men the English shot?
> ("The Man and the Echo," ll. 11–12, referring
> to *Cathleen ni Houlihan*)

As Austin Warren observes, "One might say of the early Yeats that he thought of poetry as incantation and meant the word as more than metaphor."[79] This is Yeats as "The Last Romantic," the man who felt that poetry could remake the world, that poetry had to remake the world because nothing else has freshness, power, and the ability to reawaken the ancient traditions of mankind. The task of a poet, then, is a religious task, and the poetic quest is also a religious quest. Yeats, in "The Everlasting Voices," is expressing a human reluctance to assume a formidable mystical task; he fears the burdens of the position of priest, mediator, and prophet implied in such poems as "The Poet Pleads with the Elemental Powers," first published in 1892:

The Powers, not kind like you, came where God's
    garden blows,
And stole the crimson Rose,
And hurled it from its place before His footstool white,
Into the blinding night.—
O, when shall Sorrow wander no more in the land
With Beauty hand in hand?

You great Angelic Powers of wind, and wave, and fire,
With your harmonious quire,
Encircle her I love and sing her into peace,
That my old care may cease,
And she forget the wandering and all the crimson gloom
Of the Rose in its doom.

Great Rulers of the stillness, let her no longer be
As the light on the sea,
Or as the changing spears flung by the golden stars
Out of their whirling cars,
But let a gentle silence enwrought with music flow
Where her soft footsteps go.
                    (first version, *The Bookman,* October 1892)

This poem, of course, lends itself to a direct biographical inter-
pretation, but beyond this immediate relevance, it reveals Yeats's
consciousness of his own mission as poet-seeker and his own re-
lationship with the world and the powers beyond the world. In
the original version, the poem was entitled "A Mystical Prayer
to the Masters of the Elements, Michael, Gabriel, and Raphael"
(later—1894—called Finvarra, Feacra, and Caolte). Whether
Christian or pagan names are used, Yeats felt himself empowered
to address a mystical prayer to the powers that control the basic
elements, and he had the vision to see the true spiritual state of
the world: in this early version, Yeats says that the Rose has been
removed from its proper place and the mystic Eden is gone; in
a fallen world, beauty cannot exist without sorrow.

The "she" of the poem (Maud Gonne, of course, in real life)
is, in the second stanza, involved directly with the fate of the
Rose—gloom and wandering: in other words, the cares of the
mortal world. *Doom* here seems to be used with conscious am-

biguity, combining the two meanings of "fate" and "death."
The fate of man is death, and death came into the world with
the Fall, at the same time that man became what we now call
human.

This reading is valid especially because, in later versions, the
last two lines of the second stanza are changed:

> Unfold your flaming wings and cover out of sight
> The nets of day and night.
>
> (all versions after 1894)

The phrase "nets of day and night" is very close to the "nets of
wrong and right" of "Into the Twilight." In the latter poem, as
we have seen, the terminology of "wrong and right" refers to
the middle-class world of black-and-white values. However, "day
and night" has the broader implication of this mortal world—earth—as
opposed to the eternal or immortal world. "The Poet Pleads
with the Elemental Powers," then, is a highly sophisticated
prayer; the rhythm and meter lend the feeling of an incantation.
The poet's invocation of the Powers seems part of a greater ritual
involving the poet, the lover, the Rose, and the Powers of the
universe.

In this prayer, the poet longs for the same restoration of order
and peace, the same eternal world, that Forgael searches for in
The Shadowy Waters. In a literal sense, "The Poet Pleads with
the Elemental Powers" is an incantation; *The Shadowy Waters,*
in toto, evokes the mood of ritual throughout. The speeches
sound like incantations, and every image and symbol seems
designed to create in the reader's mind the mood expressly stated
by the poet in the shorter poem.

In *The Shadowy Waters* the seeker, Forgael, has embarked on
the journey beyond the island, the true poetic quest into the un-
known. On the island, he has received an enchanted harp from
the Fool of the Wood. In the note to *Baile and Aillinn,* Yeats
identifies this harp as the harp of Aengus:

Midhir was a king of the Sidhe, or people of faery, and Etain his wife,
when driven away by a jealous woman, took refuge once upon a time with
Aengus in a house of glass, and there I have imagined her weaving harp-strings

out of Aengus' hair. I have brought the harp-strings into "The Shadowy Waters," where I interpret the myth in my own way.

(The Monthly Review, July 1902)

The Fool of the Wood is also identified with Aengus; he is the irrational element that drives men to madness. The madness here, however, is madness only to the prosaic mind. For Forgael it is enlightenment:

> No, I am not mad—
> If it be not that hearing messages
> From lasting watchers, that outlive the moon,
> At the most quiet midnight is to be stricken. . . .
> (1900 version, ll. 318-321)

Richard Ellmann observes in *The Identity of Yeats* that Yeats's note specifies that the Fool "is not *a* fool but *the* fool, 'the fool of the Rath, the fairy fool of modern Irish folklore, from whose touch no man recovers—the divine fool.' "[80] Ellmann also mentions that Yeats, in correspondence with Russell, "conjectured that the fool was associated with Aengus, god of lovers, presumably as some lower manifestation of him."[81] In the same discussion, Ellmann points out that the harp given to Forgael "is primarily, of course, the poetic imagination. . . ."[82]

The direct association of the Fool with the harp and with Aengus leads, however, to the conclusion that the madness is of a special kind, a frenzy of poetry and love. Forgael's state of mind is insanity only to those bounded by the earth.

The Shadowy Waters shows Forgael, the seeker initiated and inspired by poetic wisdom, journeying beyond the moment that has heretofore brought death or disillusion, traveling through the dream-world of growing poetic knowledge. In the first version of this dramatic poem (1900), Yeats immediately places his seeker in a world in which the natural and the supernatural are intermingled. It is a world of mist and mystery, a shadowy world through which the poet must travel. In the introductory lines, Yeats defines his position:

> I had not eyes like those enchanted eyes,
> Yet dreamed that beings happier than men
> Moved round me in the shadows, and at night
> My dreams were cloven by voices and by fires;
> And the images I have woven in this story
> Of Forgael and Dectora and the empty waters
> Moved round me in the voices and the fires;
> And more I may not write of, for them that cleave
> The waters of sleep can make a chattering tongue
> Heavy like stone, their wisdom being half silence. . . .
>
> (ll. 17–26)

The "half-silence" forced upon the poet is the mystery of the poem and makes necessary the heavy use of evocative symbols to which so many critics object.[83]

In his biography, Joseph Hone gives the following account of an early version of *The Shadowy Waters:*

> The plot of *The Shadowy Waters* had been told to George Russell when Yeats and he were still boys together at the Art School. Forgael was then a wanderer striving to escape from himself. He surprises a galley in the waters. There is a beautiful woman in the galley. He thinks that through Love he can escape from himself, and casts a magic spell on Dectora. In the original version he finds the love created by the spell is but the empty shadow of himself, and he unrolls the spell and seeks the world of the immortals alone. (cf. above, p. 73)

In the later versions of *The Shadowy Waters,* Yeats shows us a seeker who is trying to find himself in the process of his search. As in the schoolboy version, recounted to George Russell, Forgael comes upon a galleon upon which there is a woman, Dectora. Dectora, however, does not seem to be "the empty echo of the shadow of himself"; she appears, rather, as his complementary self. Forgael expects to find an immortal lover; instead, he finds a mortal like himself. The complementary nature of Forgael and Dectora is first introduced symbolically. Throughout the play, Forgael has a silver lily embroidered on his breast. When Dectora enters, led from her ship to Forgael's, she is seen to have a rose

embroidered on hers. Dectora is headed east rather than west,
but only because her own search has been futile. She states the
purpose of her abandoned search:

> Because I had hoped to come, as dreams foretold,
> Where gods are brooding in a mountainous place
> That murmurs with holy woods, and win their help
> To conquer among the countries of the north.
>   (1900 version, ll. 197–200)

Dectora's search took place within the environment of the dream,
but she was motivated by material rather than spiritual values.
The Old Sailor thinks she may be Forgael's "heart's desire" and
that the search may be at an end. However, when Forgael sees
that she is his true lover and that he should not wait for an im-
mortal lover, he sees the charming of Dectora and his union with
her as a crucial point in the search, but not as the end of the
search. As they become united, their union is symbolized by
the hair with which she covers him from the world; remaining
on Forgael's boat, she cuts the rope that binds her galley (the
materialistic search) with his, and they begin the search anew
together, as the magic harp strings cry out to the eagles. Their
spirits, united, will soar above the world of the countinghouse
as they seek their hearts' desire at the end of the world.

   Thus in Forgael and Dectora we see the union of two individu-
als into one as they embark on the last stages of the search. By
this union of two human beings, the fragmentation of the individu-
al has been resolved. Forgael and Dectora are on the last stages
of the search, yet it should be noted that they remain individuals
—they are not at this point absorbed into the universe. Unlike
Fergus, they have not experienced all things.

   The stage directions present a Pre-Raphaelite picture that
immediately evokes the mystery of the poetic journey. The
deck of a galley is revealed; the sails are decorated with three
rows of hounds from legend (the third row is the phantom hound
seen by Oisin as he embarked on his journey). To center attention
on the galley, "the sea is hidden in mist, and there is no light
except where the moon makes a brightness in the mist." Forgael
is seen sleeping; a small harp is seen beside him. In relation to

the quest, the helmsman immediately plunges in medias res, stating that Forgael has left the island for the open sea. Another sailor observes:

> How many moons have died from the full moon
> When something that was bearded like a goat
> Walked on the waters and bid Forgael seek
> His heart's desire where the world dwindles out?
> (ll. 10–13)

Forgael has been summoned to the search. His journey is not to be peaceful: within the mists of the end of the world Forgael confronts, in the persons of the sailors, the violence and conflict of ordinary men. The sailors, as spokesmen for the world of men, express doubt about Forgael's journey and threaten to kill him:

> *Forgael.* So these would have killed Forgael while
>   asleep
> Because a god has made him wise with dreams. . . .
> (ll. 25–26)

Aibric, who is mediator between the worldly doubters and the dedicated Forgael, and who still loves Forgael in spite of many doubts about his wisdom, completes the background with a picture of the journey through the world:

> No man had doubts
> When we rowed north, singing above the oars,
> And harried Alban towns, and overthrew
> The women-slingers on the Narrow Bridge,
> And passed the Outer Hebrides, and took
> Armlets of gold or shields with golden nails
> From hilly Lochlann; but our sail had passed
> Even the wandering islands of the gods,
> And heard the roar of the streams where, druids say,
> Time and the world and all things dwindle out.
> (ll. 38–47)

Forgael's reality has become the dream, and the tangible evidence of the dream is the harp:

> *Forgael.* The fool that came out of the wintry wood
> Taught me wise music, and gave me this old harp;
> And were all dreams, it would not weigh in the hand.
>
> (ll. 75-77)

The symbol of poetic inspiration is thus a physical object with weight, texture, and dimensions, an object that can be used by a man. Forgael's spiritual journey is guided and represented by a symbol that combines the physical and the spiritual.

In the symbolism and the action Yeats makes it clear that the physical and the spiritual are to be fused in poetic vision. That part of the material world represented by the sailors is to be abandoned, but the part that is true and enduring will remain. The sailors are the unimaginative world of the countinghouse, the profit-and-loss society that negates anything spiritual. Treasure, which can, as in Villiers de l'Isle-Adam's *Axel,* be a spiritual symbol, is to them a means of livelihood and a chance for retirement:

> *Second Sailor.*   And I had thought to make
> A good round sum upon this cruise, and turn—
> For I am getting on in life—to something
> That has less ups and downs than robbery.
>
> (1906 version, ll. 4-7)

Beyond this, they cannot see.

Forgael has headed toward the west into empty seas, leaving behind the world of material gain. The sailors want money and women—and through these a comfortable life; Forgael is searching for a spiritual love.

Forgael, however, cannot completely abandon the mortal world. The magic harp of Aengus is inspiring him, and its music causes visions that even the sailors can see. But, as we have seen, the harp is also a physical object. Forgael is following the man-headed birds—the souls of dead men—into the west of Celtic legend, toward the land of the immortals and of the dead. He believes, though, that he is going not to death but to immortal love. Early in the play, a dialogue between the spiritual Forgael and the practical Aibric illustrates the two interpretations of

Forgael's journey. Forgael expresses a desire to leave the physical world and enter the world of dreams. If he can get into the world of dreams, he says, he will be content and all will be well. Aibric replies that such a transition is impossible while they are "in the body" (1906 version, l. 190). Forgael is convinced that he is not being led to death, because he was promised love "as those that can outlive the moon have known it" (1906 version, l. 193). Aibric, on the other hand, feels sure that the goal is death, for

> None but the dead, or those that never lived,
> Can know that ecstasy.
> (1906 version, ll. 202-203)

Forgael states finally that it does not matter if he is going to death—for, whatever the result of his journey, he will find his love, one of the immortals.[84] To a certain extent, both Aibric and Forgael are wrong. When Forgael finds his love, she is a mortal. His reaction is dismay:

> Why are you standing with your eyes upon me?
> You are not the world's core. O no, no, no!
> . . . .
> Why do you cast a shadow?
> Where do you come from? Who brought you to this
> place?
> They would not send me one that casts a shadow.
> (1906 version, ll. 276-277, 283-285)

In the first version of the play, Dectora, like Forgael, has been engaged in a search. When he meets her, she has given up in despair:

> *Dectora.* I and that mighty king a sudden blow
> And evil fortune have overthrown sailed hither
> Because I had hoped to come, as dreams foretold,
> Where gods are brooding in a mountainous place
> That murmurs with holy woods, and win their help
> To conquer among the countries of the north.
> I have found nothing but these empty waters:
> I have turned homewards.
> (ll. 195-202)

In connection with later events of the play, the first version is
far more logical. Dectora's motivations are still material: "To
conquer among the countries of the north" (there is nothing to
indicate that this is the north of the powers of evil: more possibly
they are the same northern countries that Forgael plundered in
the early part of his voyage). But her inspiration comes from the
world of the dream. Forgael's answering speech in the first ver-
sion completes Dectora's statement and makes her later enchant-
ment by the music of the harp, their love, and the ending of the
play more meaningful:

> *Forgael.*   In the eyes of the gods,
> War-laden galleys, and armies on white roads,
> And unforgotten names, and the cold stars
> That have built all are dust on a moth's wing.
> These are their lures, but they have set their hearts
> On tears and laughter; they have lured you hither
> And lured me hither, that you might be my love.
> Aengus looks on you when I look: he awaits
> Till his Edaine, no longer a golden fly
> Among the winds, looks under pale eyelids.
> (ll. 202–211)

Forgael's corresponding speech in the later version is less explicit;
there he assumes more responsibility for gaining and keeping
Dectora:

> *Forgael.*   There are some
> That weigh and measure all in these waste seas—
> They that have all the wisdom that's in life,
> And all that prophesying images
> Made of dim gold rave out in secret tombs;
> They have it that the plans of kings and queens
> Are dust on the moth's wing; that nothing matters
> But laughter and tears—laughter, laughter, and tears;
> That every man should carry his own soul
> Upon his shoulders.
> (ll. 291–300)

A few lines later, Forgael mutters:

> When she finds out I will not let her go—
> When she knows that.
>
> (ll. 302-303)

In both versions, Dectora tries to leave but is enchanted by the harp. Also in both versions their love becomes immortal—a perfect fusion of mortal beings and immortal love. In the first version, however, Dectora's destiny is clearly linked with Forgael's through the dream. In the second, the connection is only implied: Dectora's arrival seems almost coincidence, and the charm of the harp is close to entrapment.

The fusion of mortal and immortal through love is a climactic point in the play. Forgael's acceptance of Dectora as the love destined for him by the gods is a turning point in his progress toward enlightenment; his love is not the consummation of his search, but it is a decisive step toward the goal that he outlines to Aibric:

> *Forgael.*   Where the world ends
> The mind is made unchanging, for it finds
> Miracle, ecstasy, the impossible hope,
> The flagstone under all, the fire of fires,
> The roots of the world.
> . . . .
> For it is love that I am seeking for,
> But of a beautiful, unheard-of kind
> That is not in the world.
> . . . .
> *Forgael.*   It's not a dream,
> But the reality that makes our passion
> As a lamp shadow—no—no lamp, the sun.
> What the world's million lips are thirsting for
> Must be substantial somewhere.
>
> (1906 version, ll. 100-104, 141-143, 158-162)

Since love is the dream, it is through love that Forgael can find his heart's desire.

At this point, the differences between the two versions become more significant. Allt and Alspach, in *The Variorum Edition of the Poems of W. B. Yeats,* note that between the 1900 and the 1906 versions "there is a general similarity of plot but no marked similarity of detail. The later version is longer by 188 lines and uses in whole or in part only some forty lines of the earlier."[85] Until Dectora's mention of her dream, these differences of detail have not been important to this discussion. However, from the point when Dectora falls under the spell of the harp until the last ten lines of the play (in both versions), the differences are quite relevant.

In the 1906 version, the tune of the harp causes Aibric to begin a keen for an ancient king, whom he first mistakenly identifies as Arthur, then correctly as "golden-armed Iollan," who died a thousand years before. Dectora, also under the spell, takes up the keen for Iollan. Forgael identifies himself with Iollan and sweeps Dectora up in a mood of eternal love. Later, when he says he has deceived her and has nothing for her eyes but "desolate waters and a battered ship" (l. 497), she is committed to follow him "to unimaginable happiness."

Yeats brings up the questions of reincarnation and eternity, of a keening coming perhaps from the Anima Mundi, but these problems are never developed or resolved. Yet the uncertainty creates in the reader the mood to understand Dectora's statement:

> What do I care,
> Now that my body has begun to dream,
> And you have grown to be a burning sod
> In the imagination and intellect?
> If something that's most fabulous were true—
> If you had taken me by magic spells,
> And killed a lover or husband at my feet—
> I would not let you speak, for I would know
> That it was yesterday and not to-day
> I loved him; I would cover up my ears,
> As I am doing now.
>   (ll. 485-495)

The position is now plausible: Forgael's sailors did kill Dectora's husband, and Forgael has taken her by magic spells. The world of the dream has now conquered, and Dectora is ready to reject an ivory roof and pillars of gold; she longs to knead the moon and shape it into a crown for Forgael. At the moment that love and longing assume control over her, Aibric and the sailors enter to announce their discovery of treasure. Aibric and the sailors return homeward with the treasure, while Forgael and Dectora continue onward into the mists. F. A. C. Wilson mentions the similarity between the incidents of the treasure in *The Shadowy Waters* and in *Axel*—he calls Yeats's use of treasure "a very obvious borrowing."[86] In *Axel*, the two lovers reject the earthly use of the treasure, but they do use it symbolically. In a mutual suicide at the moment of perfect bliss, they drink poison from the finest cup in the treasure. Forgael and Dectora are indifferent to the treasure, though its appearance at this particular moment gives it a symbolic value. Axel and Sara choose death, rejecting sexual experience, while Forgael and Dectora choose perfect union, whether in life or death we do not know.

It is very likely that Yeats did borrow from *Axel;* however, it is the changes that are significant. For the convenience of the reader, since the text is often difficult to obtain, I will quote at length from H. P. R. Finberg's translation of *Axel*, for which Yeats wrote an introduction. After Sara discovers the treasure, she appeals to Axel:

Yield yourself up to my enchantment! I will teach you marvellous words, heady as eastern wines. I can lull you to sleep with mortal caresses. I know the secret of infinite joys, of delicious cries, of pleasures that surpass all hope. Bury yourself in my whiteness and leave your soul there as a flower lies hidden under snow! Cover yourself with my hair and inhale the ghosts of perished roses! Yield: I will make you pale with bitterness of joy, and when you are in torment I will have mercy on you. My kiss is an ambrosial cup: the early breath of spring on the savannahs is not so warm as my breath![87]

At this moment Sara is the temptress, calling to Axel as the Voices had called Almintor:

All the favours of all other women are as nothing, set in the scale against my cruelties! I am the most sombre of maidens. I seem to remember that I have made angels fall! Alas! children and flowers have perished of my shadow.[88]

The suicide, however, comes after a purely spiritual consummation of their love, a complete rejection of the physical for the spiritual:

The quality of our hope forbids us life on earth, henceforth. What is there left for us to ask of this unhappy planet, where our sadness lingers on, save only pale reflections of such moments as these? You talk of Earth! What has it ever realized, this drop of frozen mud, whose Time is but a lie set in the face of heaven? It is this Earth, I tell you, which has become illusion! Understand me, Sara; we have destroyed in our strange hearts the love of life, and in reality are merely souls now! After this, to accept life would be mere sacrilege against ourselves. Live? Our servants will do that for us![89]

The world has become illusion, and through death Sara and Axel conquer time and preserve "this miraculous wedding night whereon, still virgins, we have yet possessed each other for all time."[90]

The Shadowy Waters, on the other hand, combines both physical and spiritual in the union of the lovers. Forgael reluctantly accepts Dectora rather than an immortal lover and, at the end of the play, he covers himself with Dectora's hair in a manner reminiscent of Sara's plea to Axel. The image of the hair, the emphasis on Dectora's mortality, and the fact that she had previously been married all clearly suggest that the consummation of this love will not be virgin.

The physical, though very much present, does not overbalance the spiritual. Dectora accepts Forgael's journey and continues with him alone across the unknown waters. The world drifts away from them and they are covered in mists. As Forgael gathers Dectora's hair about him, at the moment that the harp begins to sing aloud, he feels a growing immortality and the presence of the dream.

In the 1900 version, the total action is more enmeshed in the reality of the dream; the language is softer and the mood more evocative:

Forgael. (Going over to her) A hound that had lain
    in the red rushes
Breathed out a druid vapour, and crumbled away
The grass and the blue shadow on the stream
And the pale blossom; but I woke instead
The winds and waters to be your home for ever;
And overturned the demon with a sound
I had woven of the sleep that is in pools
Among great trees, and in the wings of owls,
And under lovers' eyelids. *(He kneels and holds
    the harp toward her.)* Bend your head
And lean your lips devoutly to this harp,
For he who gave it called it Aengus' harp
And said it was mightier than the sun and moon,
Or than the shivering casting-net of the stars.
               (ll. 278-290)

Even though the language is less direct than in the later version,
the action is more straightforward and purposeful. There is no
symbolic treasure, no keening for the dead of a thousand years,
and no deception. Iollan (spelled here *Iolan* or *Aolan*) is men-
tioned only once, and then as the subject of a tale Aibric tells
the sailors offstage. Instead, Forgael and Dectora's love is direct-
ly and continually associated with the harp and Aengus:

Forgael.   Aengus has seen
His well-beloved through a mortal's eyes;
And she, no longer blown among the winds,
Is laughing through a mortal's eyes.
               (ll. 321-324)

Like Niamh, Dectora is summoned to her love by poetry and is
thus closely associated with the symbolism of the harp:

Dectora. That crown was in my dreams—no, no—in a
    rhyme.
I know you now, beseeching hands and eyes.
I have been waiting you. A moment since
My foster-mother sang in an old rhyme
That my true love would come in a ship of pearl
Under a silken sail and silver yard,

And bring me where the children of Aengus wind
In happy dances, under a windy moon. . . .
(ll. 311-318)

Even though Forgael does not come in the ship of pearl described
in the old rhyme, Dectora sees that her meeting with Forgael is
"wiser witchcraft" (l. 320), and she accepts his love.

After they recognize their love, the movement of the play
proceeds directly toward the conclusion. Like Oisin and Niamh,
Forgael and Dectora see the supernatural red-eared hound follow-
ing a hornless deer. The sight causes them to identify and define
the love they are seeking: Forgael knows that the hound and
the deer are luring them "to the streams where the world ends"
(l. 334). Dectora, like Aibric earlier in the play, feels that death
lies at the end of the search, and that the gods are weaving nets
to ensnare them. Forgael reassures her, saying that

The fool has made
These messengers to lure men to his peace,
Where true-love wanders among the holy woods.
(ll. 335-337)

He also says that the wise fool—who has made the eternal wis-
dom (ll. 342-345)—has told him that the Immortals

. . . send their eagles
To snatch alive out of the streams all lovers
That have gone thither to look for the loud streams,
Folding their hearts' desire to their glad hearts.
(ll. 346-349)

When Dectora declares her love for Forgael, he replies that love
on earth is fleeting, deceptive, often bittersweet, composed of
"bodily tenderness" (l. 355), but that love in the place where
the world ends becomes "imperishable fire" (l. 356). As Forgael
contrasts the transitory love of earth with the eternal love turned
to "imperishable fire" found in a world of permanence (a fore-
shadowing of Yeats's later interpretation of Byzantium), Dec-
tora begins to yearn for eternal love, but she still doubts that it

can be attained. Nevertheless, she has reached a turning point in her spiritual development. Symbolically, the sailors go into the other ship, returning to the world of plunder and ale drinking they have left. Dectora now sees her past as in a dream, but she has not yet abandoned her longings for the physical world:

> I have begun remembering my dreams.
> I have commanded men in dreams. Beloved,
> We will go call these sailors, and escape
> The nets the gods have woven and our own hearts,
> And, hurrying homeward, fall upon some land
> And rule together under a canopy.
>
> (ll. 380–385)

Dectora wants Forgael's love, but she still is committed to the doubts of earth. Without the poetic inspiration that Forgael possesses, she voices the fears that Aibric and the sailors have expressed throughout the play:

> Love was not made for darkness and the winds
> That blow when heaven and earth are withering,
> For love is kind and happy. O come with me!
> Look on this body and this heavy hair;
> A stream has told me they are beautiful.
> The gods hate happiness, and weave their nets
> Out of their hatred.
>
> (ll. 394–400)

Forgael is willing to give her to Aibric and continue his search alone; he still longs for an immortal love and feels the gods are unkind for smiting him with a mortal love. Nevertheless, in spite of her misgivings and Forgael's attempts to reject her, Dectora chooses to go with Forgael, "living or dying" (l. 413). In both versions of the play, Forgael finally accepts the mortal love offered by Dectora.

The play ends ambiguously but logically. In one sense, the world of men has been rejected, but it is that part of the world represented by the sailors—the world of Saint Patrick, Paudeen, and the countinghouse that Yeats rejects throughout his career.

The mortal world is by no means both mystical and physical.
Dectora and Forgael feel that they are reaching immortality, and
they continue across unknown seas toward the west, the legendary
direction of immortality. The harp with a life of its own signifies
renewed poetic inspiration and approval of the gods, and the
crown Dectora places on Forgael's head becomes a visual image
of spiritual achievement and success. Nevertheless, the image is
made somewhat ambiguous because Forgael is crowned by the
mortal lover rather than by a spiritual or supernatural power. The
actions of the lovers, though intended to isolate them from the
world, are definitely physical: the arms and hair are, as discussed
above, highly suggestive. There is no question of a suicide pact
here. The suggestion is that the artist needs a certain degree of
isolation, but that he should not totally abandon the world for
which he creates—the same idea expressed by Yeats earlier in
his use of the rose and later in his use of the tower.

The conclusion of *The Shadowy Waters* emphasizes more than
anything else a union of physical and spiritual, mortal and im-
mortal. Forgael may find that the love destined for him is not
immortal, but mortal, but he also finds mortal love leading him
to immortality. At the moment that Forgael and Dectora accept
their common destiny, the harp of inspiration signifies hope for
the outcome of the voyage. Mortality, immortality, poetry, and
the dream are all essential to each other in the poetic quest.
Forgael has been mystically initiated as an artist and is now
worthy to continue his quest beyond the island into the world
of the unknown.

If *The Shadowy Waters* is seen as a poem and an elaboration
of the poetic quest, the vagueness and the ambiguities become
necessary to the concern of the play and are no longer regarded
as cumbersome embroidery. From this point of view, many
problems disappear. A good example of the frustration experi-
enced by some readers can be seen in the criticism of Leonard
Nathan, who sees *The Shadowy Waters* as a partial failure from
a dramatic standpoint. He objects to the "multiplicity of symbols"
that, "because of their obscurity or their ornamental value, do
not function to advance or deepen the intention of the play."[91]
He complains that the plot "gives no sense of movement," and
he quotes Parkinson's objections to the lyric style of the play

and the lack of variety in the characters.[92] Nathan goes on to discuss at length what he feels to be the fundamental weakness of the play. He feels that Yeats was unsure both of his theme and of the nature of the supernatural. He compares the play unfavorably with *Axel.* The theme of both plays is "the quest of the mortal for the immortal"—"the attempt of human love to transform itself into spiritual love through a pure, intense union." According to Nathan's argument, Axel and Sara were confident of their destiny: they knew that their union required death or something closely akin to death. Yeats's play, on the other hand, is governed by vagueness and uncertainty.[93] In addition, according to Nathan, the play fails as tragic drama. He mentions the warnings to Forgael that the intentions of the gods are deceitful and observes that "this warning note is buried under a constant flow of what might be termed Forgael's rhetoric of certitude." According to this interpretation, Forgael has misinterpreted the oracle of the gods—the fool—and he is destined for a tragic end such as befell Macbeth or Oedipus. Nathan says that "the climactic resolution, the hero's doom, is missing from the play" (p. 76). Because Yeats would not clarify his position, and because Forgael was given no clear opposition, "the tragic pattern is not allowed to take clear shape and complete itself."[94]

Nathan does see a certain value in *The Shadowy Waters* as a long lyrical poem; and like Ellmann, he appreciates the use of symbolism in dramatic poetry. It is, in fact, precisely within these areas that *The Shadowy Waters* succeeds, and any attempts to force it into other molds are bound to fail. F. A. C. Wilson takes a far more fruitful approach when he examines *The Shadowy Waters* as symbolic drama in contrast to *Deirdre.* He examines the symbols in *The Shadowy Waters* and states that

The play . . . is an elaborate study of the relation between love and the visionary world; and it tends always toward archetypal stasis and away from the minute particulars of life. The characters are prototypes for all humanity: they are not individuals.[95]

An interpretation like Professor Wilson's uses only that which the play contains, and allows the actions and symbols a full range of suggestiveness. However, in the same discussion Wilson proceeds to damn the play for what he regards as its conventional structure modeled on five-act tragedy, its "orthodox plot," and resultant "lethargy."[96]

It is difficult to see *The Shadowy Waters* as a play that should have been a tragedy or, indeed, as anything other than what it is: a lyrical symbolic drama. As a conventional tragedy, *The Shadowy Waters* does fail, simply because it is not a tragedy. Its outcome is not tragic and can never be tragic. The ending of a tragedy is suffering and death. Nathan's examples of *Oedipus Rex* and *Oedipus at Colonus* are excellent for illustration. In *Oedipus Rex,* Oedipus comes to recognize his hubris and to punish himself for his sins. In *Oedipus at Colonus,* Oedipus achieves a type of redemption and his life ends in a way that is certainly mystical. These plays, however, are based on a view of life, time, and death, of man's position in the universe, that Yeats does not share.

Forgael's relationship with the universe is quite different from that of Oedipus. Forgael does not see himself in conflict with the gods, and there is no proof that his interpretation of the message of the fool and the harp is a mistake or error. We have no real grounds for construing Forgael's sense of mission as hubris, for nowhere in the play do we have a scene that corresponds with the Greek "recognition scene," nor is there any real indication that there should be one. There is no dramatic irony in connection with Forgael's mission: the reader (or audience) actually has less knowledge than Forgael. The doubts and warnings of which Nathan makes so much are all voiced by those who speak for the material world—never by Forgael or any representative of the gods. If there is a Tiresias here, it is Forgael himself.

Forgael knows he is headed toward the end of the world where time burns out. He also knows that the grey birds he is following are the souls of dead men, but Yeats does not say specifically whether Forgael is following them to death or to some form of life. Whichever it may be, Forgael is undaunted; even if the end is death, it is death to the material world but not to the spirit. He is confident that he will find perfect love and "what the world's million lips are thirsting for." He is as one with the souls of the dead who are also on a journey and who are similarly confident of their destination—immortality and happiness. At one point in the play, Forgael overhears their voices, as two birds hover in the air waiting for another:

> "How light we are now we are changed to birds!"
> And the other answers, "Maybe we shall find
> Our hearts' desire now that we are so light."
>   (1900 version, ll. 143–145)

When the third one comes, she cries out:

> "I have fled to my beloved
> In the waste air. I will wander by his side
> Among the windy meadows of the dawn."
>   (1900 version, ll. 151–153)

These birds are Forgael's guides, and their longings and aspirations are an exact parallel to his. There is a striking parallel between the "laggard" fleeing to her beloved and Dectora, the seeker who has abandoned the search, meeting with Forgael, who is waiting for the love the gods will send him.

The ambiguities of death and life indicate that the distinction, at least in the conventional sense, is irrelevant for Forgael and, finally, for Dectora. To use Wilson's terminology, they are certain that love is a part of the visionary world, and, in the tradition of other mystics, they are prepared to undergo whatever experiences will unite them eternally.

Wilson's term "archetypal stasis" (in spite of its connotations) is close to the true meaning of the play. It is from the symbolic structure and the plot—the very lack of movement of which Nathan speaks—that *The Shadowy Waters* derives its meaning. The stillness of the drama indicates that Forgael has reached a certain plateau in his mystical and poetic progress; the departure of Aibric and the sailors, the isolation of Dectora and Forgael, the harp, the boat, and the sea, symbolically define his stage of poetic development.

The meanings of the major symbols in *The Shadowy Waters* have already been discussed. No attempt will be made to cover them completely, for this is impossible. The symbols are fluid and evocative, and their evocations will change to a greater or lesser extent with each individual reader. A discussion of the meaning of the stillness or nonaction of the play, however, will help clarify the relation of the symbols to the plot and will elucidate the meaning of the play and, indirectly, of the other works under discussion. The nonaction here is merely a suspension of action: the knowledge that a journey is under way is constantly kept in the foreground. This relation of action and nonaction is central to all the poems under discussion and, indeed, to the Celtic Twilight itself. The island, for example, like Forgael's "stasis," is a temporary state of being in a process of becoming, a brief earthly shadow of the state of true being or unity to which the poet aspires.

The term "spiritual quest" has been used throughout this study interchangeably with other terms such as "poetic quest." "Spiritual quest" and "poetic quest" are often the same—and for a good reason. Poetry, Yeats tells us, is true religion, and, as in Blake, poetry and mysticism are combined in the inspired poet, the one who has been touched by the Sidhe. For this reason, Forgael's stage in poetic development can be seen through an analogy with the spiritual life of a mystic (provided, of course, the analogy is not pressed too far).

Classically, there is a threefold division of the spiritual life into the Purgative, Illuminative, and Unitive ways.[97] These divisions are further subdivided in the writings of various mystics such as Saint Teresa of Jesus and Saint John of the Cross, each with certain individual differences. All, though, are aimed at the Unitive Way, in which the individual mystic achieves a state of unity with God and the universe, and at the Beatific Vision of God, in which mortal man comes as close as he can to a state of pure being. The Unitive Way corresponds directly to Yeats's Unity of Being; both designate states of being in which man becomes one with the universe, in which, while seeming to transcend life, man becomes more a part of life than he ever before believed possible. The isolated poet, like the isolated mystic, must seek his own path; his may be similar to that of other poets, and his inspiration may also resemble theirs, but his art is unique. His inspiration may seem to set him apart from other men, and it may lead him to a state of unity, yet he remains a man and of the world of men. As he grows in poetic illumination, his spiritual life grows in both worlds, uniting man with God and God with man.

Forgael's poetic faith has taken him through purgation. He is still in the process of illumination, still in the state of becoming, but closer to the state of pure being where "time and the world and all things dwindle out" (1900 version, l. 47). Unlike Saint John of the Cross, he cannot tell of the Unitive Way: this he has not yet achieved. He can, however, tell of the temptations and doubts that have assailed him, and of the faith that has sustained him.

Some earlier seekers, like the Old Knight and Oisin, were conquered by time and death. The Witch Vivien, who felt herself to be immortal, was defeated by time. Other seekers—Almintor, Kanva, Fergus, and Mongan—were burdened by impending death, artistic immortality, or the remembrance of many lives. King Goll was driven to madness. Over all these figures there is a shadow not felt or seen by Dectora and Forgael. Forgael has a greater awareness of his role as a poet and visionary, and he accepts the burdens of the wisdom and isolation of the poet with greater assurance, confidence, and understanding.

When Yeats's poetry is discussed, as it must be, in terms of life, death, time, mortality, and immortality, a proper perspective requires an awareness that Yeats's ultimate concern is poetic. He is not attempting to formulate a philosophy in very clearly defined terms; he works on suggestion rather than definition, on feelings and imagination rather than reason.

Yeats is the isolated artist in many ways. In his personal life, he was emphatically Irish, but never learned Gaelic; he was a religious Western European, but not a Christian. His sources and influences are many and varied, but often quite inconsistent with each other, being sometimes scholarly, sometimes esoteric, sometimes popular, and sometimes downright eccentric. Yet, like any man, he was not in total isolation; and, like any writer, he has certain affinities with other writers. Much could be done, for example, with the connections between Yeats and the English Romantic poets, primarily Wordsworth, Shelley, and Keats; for the purposes of this discussion, however, a few observations must suffice.

The Shadowy Waters, The Wanderings of Oisin, and the other

poems discussed in this study evolved out of the Romantic tradi-
tion; and the ambiguities of life, death, happiness, and sorrow
are quite similar to those found in Keats by Frank Kermode, in
The Romantic Image, and Robert Graves, in *The White Goddess*
(concerning the goddess Moneta in "Hyperion" and La Belle
Dame sans Merci). The same case could be made for Yeats that
Kermode and Graves make for Keats.[98] As we have seen, the
poems about the poetic search, beginning with *The Island of
Statues* and *The Seeker,* all involve the attainment of a higher
poetic knowledge, and this vision of knowledge contains the
paradoxes represented by Moneta and La Belle Dame, who can
be love, death, poetry, joy, and suffering, all at once. The func-
tion of the island and the transformation of the king are striking-
ly reflected in Yeats. Such generalizations, however, can be
carried only so far. Moneta and La Belle Dame can be seen as
manifestations of the ancient goddess, but ultimately they are
personal goddesses with immediate and specific relevance to
Keats. Though religious and mythic approaches, like the historical
and biographical, can often give the critic some valuable insights
into the poetry, these insights can become, as in Morton Seiden's
and some of F. A. C. Wilson's work, almost more important than
the poetry itself and can thus lead to a complete distortion of
the poem as a work of art.

In the case of *The Shadowy Waters*—and similar arguments
could be made for any of the works discussed above—the total
meaning is not to be found in comparisons with so-called "con-
ventional" or "orthodox" drama, nor with Christian mysticism
or ancient myths. This poem is a dramatic presentation of what
Frank Kermode calls the "Romantic Image": the play itself is
an image with the same meaning that Kermode sees in the Dancer:

 For this Dancer is one of Yeats's great reconciling images, containing life
in death, death in life, movement and stillness, action and contemplation,
body and soul; in fact all that passionate integrity that was split and destroyed
when Descartes, as Yeats puts it, discovered that he could think better in his
bed than out of it.[99]

The Shadowy Waters can be seen as a total image, each
action and symbol being a part of a complex but unified structure.

The tension between action and nonaction reconciles the opposites of action and contemplation, which, as Kermode says, "is the purpose of the Yeatsian symbol."[100] Underlying this basic tension of action and contemplation, there are other tensions that give it richer and deeper significance. There is the tension between the artist in isolation and the artist among his fellow men; the tension between man and the gods; the tensions of mortal and immortal love, of waking and sleeping, of life and death, of the states of becoming and being.

Forgael is the artist in isolation, in conflict with those who both fail to understand and even fear his art (the sailors), and with those who love and try to understand, but fail (Aibric). He is confronted with both his nature as an inspired poet and his relation to mortal and immortal love. Forgael's problems with the love relationship reveal that he does not fully understand the nature of his role, but it is equally clear that he accepts his destiny as an inspired artist. His inspiration, the harp, resolves for him the tensions of life and death, becoming and being.[101]

Forgael's wisdom, though, can never be seen by the sailors and Aibric. In this sense, Forgael is the modern artist whose world does not see him as a powerful man inspired by the gods. All but Forgael interpret the inspiration as malignant design; from the earthly point of view, perhaps, the gods are perverse, and since Aengus needs earthly lovers to realize his own love, he may be leading Forgael and Dectora to death. The sailors can understand no more than this. But there is more.

In Yeats's long poem *Baile and Aillinn,* the lovers united by Aengus have attained wisdom, love, and happiness higher and more perfect than that of mortal man. As has been noted before, their death is anything but tragic: it is a fulfillment. Since Forgael could never make the sailors comprehend a love such as this, the tensions of *The Shadowy Waters* are resolved only when the sailors return to the harsh light of the world and Forgael and Dectora go on into the mists of the dream.

The reconciliation is ultimately seen in the person of the artist, Forgael, and secondarily through the use of image and suggestion. Throughout the play, suggestions and images of physical weight are delicately balanced with suggestions of lightness and weightlessness. The significance of the harp was mentioned before: it is a gift from the supernatural; yet, Forgael uses its physical weight as proof of its existence and the reality of his quest. The souls of the dead refer to their lightness in a passage already quoted, and their comparative weightlessness is in direct contrast to the physical weight of Forgael and Dectora. Even the boat itself, buoyed up on the sea, contributes to the total effect of the contrast, as does the physical solidity of the boat and sails with the shifting incorporeality of the mists. Throughout the play, and significantly at the end, Yeats sustains the presence of solidity and lightness, illustrating the fact that physical and spiritual both are necessary to the poetic quest.

The spiritual and physical are effectively combined in Forgael: he has his inspiration and his mission from the gods. At the end of the play, he is left with only those elements of the physical world that are of value to him: his love, his boat, and his harp, all of which, in themselves, combine the physical and the spiritual. The grossly material has been abandoned, and Forgael can now continue his quest for the goal of the true artist.

CHAPTER SEVEN

THE ENDLESS QUEST

The mood, theme, and significance of the poetic quest are beautifully summarized by Yeats himself in a lyric first published in 1897, "The Song of Wandering Aengus." Using the first person, Aengus very simply and very musically tells of his wandering search.

In the first stanza, Aengus relates the beginning of his quest:

> I went out to the hazel wood
> Because a fire was in my head,
> And cut and peeled a hazel wand,
> And hooked a berry to a thread. . . .
> (ll. 1–4)

The summons itself is not mentioned, but it is clear that Aengus is inspired. He prepares himself for fishing *because* a fire was in his head. He puts the berry in a stream and catches a silver trout.

In the second stanza, Aengus reveals that his inspired actions have put him in contact with the spiritual world. He puts the trout on the floor, turns to blow on the fire, and hears a rustling sound from the floor behind him. The fish "had become a glimmering girl" (l. 13); she calls him by his name, runs out, and fades "through the brightening air" (l. 16).

In the third stanza, we find that Aengus is telling his story from the perspective of age. He is "old with wandering" (l. 17), and he is still seeking the glimmering girl and an immortal love. When he finds the girl, Aengus will "kiss her lips and take her hands" (l. 20); he will "walk among long dappled grass" (l. 21) and pluck the apples of the moon and sun—the apples of silver and of gold.

The structure of the poem, the repetitions and sounds of the words, the highly articulated rhymes, all provide the atmosphere of the dream. The ethereal beauty of the poem and the almost ritualized actions, especially in the first two stanzas, involve the reader in a state of vision in which he can feel and share the significance of Aengus's experience.

There is a strong tension here. Within the quiet movement and the pastoral landscape, Aengus is inspired to the point of madness—the poem was even entitled "Mad Song" in its first printing—but this is the same madness that the sailors see in Forgael, not the madness of King Goll. The "fire in his head" inspires Aengus and causes him to perform the actions that determine the nature of his existence. He goes fishing, as if he were performing a ritual, and it is through this ritual act that the spiritual world is contacted. The trout he catches—one of the Tuatha De Danaan, Yeats tells us in a note—becomes the glimmering girl who summons him to the search. After the girl calls his name, Aengus wanders in an ambiguous and half-understood relationship between the physical and the spiritual. In his wanderings over the earth, he is longing for the love of the supernatural girl and for the eternity symbolized by the silver and gold apples of the last two lines.

In essence, "The Song of Wandering Aengus" is a lyric statement of the poetic quest. Aengus is presented in the mortal state of becoming, searching and longing for pure being. His wanderings are dreamlike, to all outward appearances erratic and aimless; yet he, like the other seekers, is conscious of a goal and a purpose for his wanderings.

In the last stanza, Aengus's vision of the goal is described, and through this description Aengus defines true being and true reality—the state in which mortal and immortal, physical and spiritual, are fused in perfect existence. The cluster of pictures in the last six lines—Aengus's kissing his loved one's lips, holding her hand, walking through the grass, and plucking the gold and silver apples—creates in the reader's mind the meaning of true reality; the love combines mortal and immortal. The object is immortal, but the actions are those of earth. The silver and gold apples suggest the richness and permanence of precious metal; their material also suggests the craftsmanship of the artist —the goldsmith of Yeats's later Byzantium concept. Their association with moon and sun, and Aengus's actions in plucking them, seem to indicate a reconciliation of opposites, even on a celestial scale, as sun and moon are joined together in the one action of fruit-gathering.

It should be mentioned however, that the artificial nature of the apples is not emphasized here as it is in the case of the golden bird in "Sailing to Byzantium":

> Once out of nature I shall never take
> My bodily form from any natural thing,
> But such a form as Grecian goldsmiths make. . . .
> (ll. 25-27)

The total meaning of the last lines of "The Song of Wandering Aengus" suggests, rather, the combination of art and nature that Yeats emphasizes throughout the earlier poetry. The landscape of earth is here transformed, but it is by no means obliterated. In the apples the objects of nature are made permanent, while, in direct contrast, Aengus will "walk through the dappled grass," kissing the lips and taking the hand of his beloved. The state described here is one that simultaneously embraces permanence and impermanence, action and contemplation.

There is also in this poem a hint of the concern with time that is found throughout Yeats's poetry. Aengus will pluck the apples "till time and times are done" (l. 22). On one level, this is a beautifully phrased way of saying "forever." Yet the very meaning of the words, the connotations of "tell," "time," "done," would indicate that Yeats's phrase is roughly equivalent to the liturgical *per omnia saecula saeculorum,* which is rendered in the English Book of Common Prayer as "world without end." The eternal state, in other words, can be indicated only in terms of earth and is, in some mysterious way, subject to the conditions of earth. Never in Yeats, and, one might add, never even in Byzantium, can the earth be totally rejected.

In describing the poetic quest, "The Song of Wandering Aengus" also describes the environment in which Yeats himself was working. The quest is not just a patterned series of actions in which we can find all sorts of connotations, ranging from the archetypal Grail quest theory propounded by F. A. C. Wilson for some of Yeats's work, to a biographical—and even Freudian— relation to the poet's life, as proposed by Morton Seiden, to the poetic theory developed here. The poetic quest is a concern and a milieu, both poetic and religious, in which the inspired poet works and searches and hopes, and in which the poet truly becomes the maker, creating something that becomes more than its creator. As Yeats himself observed concerning another artist's work:

The emotion which a work of art awakens in an onlooker has commonly little to do with the deliberate purpose of its maker, and must vary with every onlooker. Every artist who has any imagination builds better than he knows.[102]

And Yeats, throughout his career, continued the search, following in his own way the wanderers who had gone before him. As he says in "The Secret Rose":

> . . . the proud dreaming king who flung the crown
> And sorrow away, and calling bard and clown
> Dwelt among wine-stained wanderers in deep woods;
> And him who sold tillage, and house, and goods,
> And sought through lands and islands numberless years,
> Until he found, with laughter and with tears,
> A woman of so shining loveliness
> That men threshed corn at midnight by a tress,
> A little stolen tress. I, too, await
> The hour of thy great wind of love and hate.
> When shall the stars be blown about the sky,
> Like the sparks blown out of a smithy, and die?
> Surely thine hour has come, thy great wind blows,
> Far-off, most secret, and inviolate Rose?

NOTES

1. See Graham Hough, *The Last Romantics* (London: Methuen, 1961); Arthur Symons, *The Symbolist Movement in Literature* (New York: Dutton, 1958); William Butler Yeats, *Autobiographies* (London: Macmillan, 1955). Since many critical works on Yeats have been recently reprinted, either in revised hardbacks or in paperback editions, whenever possible, for the convenience of the reader, the most recent edition, whether hardback or paper, has been cited. In the Bibliography, the date of the first edition is given in parenthesis.

2. See Balachandra Rajan, *W. B. Yeats: A Critical Introduction* (London: Hutchinson University Library, 1965), p. 13; and Donald Davie, "Yeats, the Master of a Trade," in Denis Donoghue, ed., *The Integrity of Yeats* (Cork: Mercier Press for Radio Éireann, 1964), p. 65.

3. "Yeats, the Public Man," in Donoghue, *Integrity*, p. 23.

4. Eleanor Terry Lincoln, ed., *Pastoral and Romance: Modern Essays in Criticism* (Englewood Cliffs, N. J.: Prentice-Hall, 1969), Intro., pp. 2-3.

5. "Yeats's Symbolism," in Donoghue, *Integrity*, p. 34.

6. Reprinted in Peter Allt and Russell K. Alspach, eds., *The Variorum Edition of the Poems of W. B. Yeats* (New York: Macmillan, 1957), p. 800. All of the quotations from Yeats's poetry are from this edition, which also includes the notes to the poems.

7. *W. B. Yeats: Man and Poet* (London: Routledge, 1962), p. 121.

8. Comte Villiers de l'Isle-Adam, *Axel* (trans. by H. P. R. Finberg; Preface by W. B. Yeats; London: Jarrolds, 1925), Preface, p. 7.

9. Arthur Symons, *The Symbolist Movement in Literature* (New York: Dutton, 1958), pp. 2-3.

10. *W. B. Yeats and Tradition* (New York: Macmillan, 1958), p. 37.

11. See Denis Donoghue, *William Butler Yeats* (New York: Viking, 1971), pp. 19 ff.

12. Lady Augusta Gregory, *Poets and Dreamers* (London: John Murray, 1902), p. 60.

13. *William Butler Yeats: The Poet as Mythmaker 1865-1939* (Lansing: Michigan State University Press, 1962), p. 9.

14.   *The Poetry of W. B. Yeats* (London: Oxford University Press, 1941), p. 53.

15.   *The Works of Morris and of Yeats in Relation to Early Saga Literature* (Cambridge: Cambridge University Press, 1937), p. 141.

16.   *Man and Poet,* p. 76.

17.   W. B. Yeats, *Memoirs* (London: Macmillan, 1972), pp. 123-124.

18.   Quoted in Seiden, *Poet as Mythmaker,* p. 79.

19.   Roger McHugh, ed., *W. B. Yeats Letters to Katherine Tynan* (Dublin: Clonmore and Reynolds, 1953), pp. 181-182.

20.   *W. B. Yeats: A Critical Study* (New York: Dodd, Mead, 1915), p. 25.

21.   Quoted from the definitive edition (1949). The thought is essentially the same in all versions.

22.   See Hoare, *Morris and Yeats,* pp. 111-117 and passim.

23.   *Yeats,* p. 42.

24.   *Yeats,* p. 43.

25.   *Yeats,* p. 44.

26.   See, for example, Seiden, *Poet as Mythmaker;* Virginia Moore, *The Unicorn: William Butler Yeats' Search for Reality* (New York: Macmillan, 1954), passim; and W. B. Yeats's letters to Katherine Tynan.

27.   *Yeats's Iconography* (New York: Macmillan, 1960), p. 248.

28.   Donoghue, *Integrity,* pp. 47-48.

29.   See, for a sampling of critics disturbed by the early poetry, Dorothy Hoare, *Morris and Yeats,* p. 141 and passim; Morton Seiden, *Poet as Mythmaker,* p. 287; Norman Jeffares, *Man and Poet,* p. 121; J. Middleton Murry and R. P. Blackmur in James Hall and Martin Steinmann, eds., *The Permanence of Yeats* (New York: Collier, 1961), pp. 9-13, 38-59.

30.   See Harold Bloom, *Yeats* (New York: Oxford University Press, 1970), pp. 62, 64-66, and passim.

31.   See Ellmann, *The Man and the Masks,* p. 276.

32.   W. B. Yeats, *Autobiographies* (London: Macmillan, 1955), p. 499.

33.   W. B. Yeats, ed., *Beltaine: The Organ of the Irish Literary Theatre,* I, 1 (May, 1899), 7.

34.   T. W. Rolleston, *Myths and Legends of the Celtic Race* (London: Harrap, 1911), p. 90.

35.   "Wisdom and Dreams," ll. 5-8. (published in *The Bookman,* December, 1893; reprinted in the *Variorum Edition,* p. 743).

36.   *Autobiographies,* p. 291.

37.   In John Unterecker, ed., *Yeats: A Collection of Critical Essays* (Englewood Cliffs: Prentice-Hall, 1963), p. 80.

38.   In Unterecker, *Yeats,* p. 86.

39.   "Quest," Unterecker, *Yeats,* p. 86.

40.   "Quest," Unterecker, *Yeats,* p. 87.

41.   Roger McHugh, ed., *W. B. Yeats Letters to Katherine Tynan,* p. 47. Clonmore and Reynolds, 1953), p. 47.

42.   Louis MacNeice, *The Poetry of W. B. Yeats* (London: Oxford University Press for University of New Hampshire, 1941), p. 61.

43.   Wilson, *Yeats's Iconography,* p. 111.

44.   "Quest," Unterecker, *Yeats,* p. 85.

45.   "Quest," Unterecker, *Yeats,* p. 85.

46.   Jeffares, *Man and Poet,* p. 73.

47. See Yeats, *Autobiographies*, pp. 71-73.
48. Ursula Bridge, ed., *W. B. Yeats and T. Sturge Moore: Their Correspondence* (London: Routledge and Kegan Paul, 1953), p. 13.
49. Yeats, *Autobiographies*, pp. 171-172.
50. Erwin Panofsky, "Et in Arcadia Ego," from *Philosophy and History: Essays Presented to Ernst Cassirer* (Oxford: Clarendon Press), pp. 295-320. Reprinted in Lincoln, ed., *Pastoral and Romance*, pp. 25-46.
51. *The Unicorn: William Butler Yeats' Search for Reality* (New York: Macmillan, 1954), p. 47.
52. *A Literary History of Ireland from Earliest Times to the Present Day* (London: Fisher Unwin, 1906), pp. 82-84.
53. *Literary History*, p. 84.
54. *Literary History*, p. 89.
55. Douglas Hyde, *The Story of Early Gaelic Literature* (London: Fisher Unwin, 1920), p. 48.
56. *Ideas of Good and Evil*, in *Essays and Introductions* (London: Macmillan, 1961), pp. 158-159.
57. W. B. Yeats, "Where There is Nothing," in *Mythologies* (London: Macmillan, 1958), pp. 189-190.
58. Joseph Hone, *W. B. Yeats 1865-1939* (New York: St. Martin's Press, 1962), p. 166.
59. Leonard E. Nathan, *The Tragic Drama of William Butler Yeats: Figures in a Dance* (New York: Columbia University Press, 1965), p. 5.
60. P. 13, for example. See also Richard Ellmann, *Yeats: The Man and the Masks* (New York: Dutton-Everyman, 1958), p. 36.
61. J. E. Circlot, *A Dictionary of Symbols* (New York: Philosophical Library, 1962), p. 39.
62. Circlot, *Symbols*, p. 39.
63. Some critics, however, do see a war between the natural and supernatural. See, for example, Ellmann, *Masks*, p. 36; Nathan, *Drama*, p. 3; and Colin Wilson, *The Strength to Dream: Literature and the Imagination* (Boston: Houghton Mifflin, 1962), p. 15.
64. Thomas Parkinson, *W. B. Yeats Self-Critic* (Berkeley and Los Angeles: University of California Press, 1951), p. 12.
65. Alex Zwerdling, *Yeats and the Heroic Ideal* (New York: New York University Press, 1965), p. 50.
66. Seiden, *Poet as Mythmaker*, p. 55.
67. Seiden, *Poet as Mythmaker*, pp. 55-56.
68. Reprinted in the *Variorum Edition*, p. 793.
69. See Myles Dillon, *Early Irish Literature* (Chicago: University of Chicago Press, 1943), pp. 101-131.
70. See Dillon, *Early Irish*, pp. 101-131.
71. William Morris, *The Earthly Paradise* (London: Longmans, Green, 1896), Vol. 1, p. 3.
72. *Autobiographies*, p. 90.
73. *Autobiographies*, p. 150.
74. *Autobiographies*, p. 183.
75. *Man and Poet*, p. 91.
76. Reprinted in the *Variorum Edition*, p. 842.
77. W. B. Yeats, *A Vision* (New York: Macmillan, 1961), pp. 279-280.

78. An Ollave in ancient Ireland was a learned man; in the first version of the poem (1887), Yeats had "Druid" for "Ollave," and in two other earlier versions (1888 and 1889), he simply had "old man." The idea of Druid, however, seems to be implied in all versions.

79. "William Butler Yeats: the Religion of a Poet," *Rage for Order* (Ann Arbor: University of Michigan Press, 1959), p. 66.

80. Richard Ellmann, *The Identity of Yeats* (New York: Oxford University Press, 1964), p. 82.

81. P. 82. See also Nathan, *Drama,* p. 70.

82. *Identity,* p. 82.

83. See, for example, Leonard Nathan and Thomas Parkinson.

84. *Shadowy Waters* (1906 version), ll. 177–213.

85. Editors' notes, p. 220.

86. *Tradition,* p. 39.

87. Adam, *Axel,* p. 260.

88. Adam, *Axel,* p. 260.

89. Adam, *Axel,* p. 284.

90. Adam, *Axel,* p. 285.

91. Nathan, *Drama,* p. 72.

92. Nathan, *Drama,* pp. 72–73.

93. Nathan, *Drama,* pp. 74–75.

94. Nathan, *Drama,* p. 76.

95. *Tradition,* pp. 38–39.

96. *Tradition,* p. 39.

97. See E. W. Trueman Dicken, *The Crucible of Love: A Study of the Mysticism of Saint Teresa of Jesus and Saint John of the Cross* (London: Darton, Longman and Todd, 1963), p. 224.

98. See Frank Kermode, *Romantic Image* (New York: Vintage, 1964), p. 9; and Robert Graves, *The White Goddess: A Historical Grammar of Poetic Myth* (New York: Noonday, 1966), pp. 431–432.

99. *Romantic Image,* p. 48.

100. *Romantic Image,* p. 43.

101. See Circlot's brief discussion of the symbolism of the harp in *Symbols,* p. 133.

102. *Beltaine,* I, 2 (September, 1899), 21.

SELECTED BIBLIOGRAPHY

WORKS OF W. B. YEATS

(For a complete listing, see Allen Wade, ed., *A Bibliography of the Writings of W. B. Yeats*, London, 1958.)

The definitive edition of the poems is *The Poems of W. B. Yeats* (2 vols.), London, 1949.

The more readily accessible edition is *The Collected Poems of W. B. Yeats*, London, 1950.

The student of Yeats will find most useful Peter Allt and Russell E. Alspach, eds., *The Variorum Edition of the Poems of W. B. Yeats*, New York: Macmillan, 1957. This edition, using the two-volume definitive edition as the text, contains in addition to the poems of the definitive edition all other poems by Yeats, all variant readings, a complete bibliography, and a collation of all the notes and prefaces to the various editions of the poems.

Most of the plays are published in one volume, *The Collected Plays of W. B. Yeats*, London, 1952.

The most readily accessible edition of the prose works is that which has been published by Macmillan:
Autobiographies. London, 1955.
Essays and Introductions. London, 1961.
Explorations. London, 1962.
Mythologies. London, 1958.
A Vision. New York, 1961.

Yeats's Journal and the first draft of his Autobiography are now available in W. B. Yeats, *Memoirs* (transcribed and edited by Denis Donoghue), London: Macmillan, 1972.

Since some of the prose, such as the early novels *John Sherman* and *Dhoya*, is not available in the volumes listed above, the following editions were also used:

The Collected Works in Verse and Prose of William Butler Yeats (8 vols.). London: Shakespeare Head, 1908.

Yeats, W. B., ed. *Irish Fairy and Folk Tales.* New York: Modern Library, n.d.

–––, ed. *Beltaine: The Organ of the Irish Literary Theatre.* I, 1–3 (1899–1900). Pub. in 1 vol., London: Sign of the Unicorn, 1900.

The standard edition of the letters is Allan Wade, ed., *The Letters of W. B. Yeats,* London: Rupert Hart-Davis, 1954.

Other editions used in this study are:

Bax, Clifford, ed. *Florence Farr, Bernard Shaw, W. B. Yeats: Letters.* London: Home and Von Thal, 1946.

Bridge, Ursula, ed. *W. B. Yeats and T. Sturge Moore: Their Correspondence.* London: Routledge and Kegan Paul, 1953.

McHugh, Roger, ed. *W. B. Yeats Letters to Katherine Tynan.* Dublin: Clonmore and Reynolds, 1953.

Wellesley, Dorothy, ed. *Letters on Poetry from W. B. Yeats to Dorothy Wellesley.* London: Oxford University Press, 1940.

SECONDARY SOURCES CITED OR DIRECTLY USED

Abrams, M. H. *The Mirror and the Lamp: Romantic Theory and the Critical Tradition.* New York: Norton, 1958 (1st ed., 1953).

Adam, Comte Villiers de l'Isle. *Axel.* Trans. H. P. R. Finberg, with intro. by W. B. Yeats. London: Jarrolds, 1925.

Beltaine: The Organ of the Irish Literary Theatre. ed. W. B. Yeats. I, 1–3 (1899–1900) (pub. in 1 vol. London: Sign of the Unicorn, 1900).

Bjersby, Birgit. *The Interpretation of the Cuchulain Legend in the Works of W. B. Yeats.* Upsala Irish Studies, no. 1. Upsala, 1950.

Bloom, Harold. *Yeats.* New York: Oxford University Press, 1970.

Bulwer-Lytton. *Zanoni.* London: Routledge and Son, 1878.

Campbell, J. J. *Legends of Ireland.* London: Batsford, 1955.

Circlot, J. E. *A Dictionary of Symbols.* New York: Philosophical Library, 1962.

Clark, Sir Kenneth. "Art and Society," *Harper's,* CCXXIII (August, 1961), 74–82.

Curtis, Edmund. *A History of Ireland* (1st ed., 1936). London: Methuen, 1961.

Dicken, E. W. Trueman. *The Crucible of Love: A Study of the Mysticism of Saint Teresa of Jesus and Saint John of the Cross.* London: Darton, Longman and Todd, 1963.

Dillon, Myles. *Early Irish Literature.* Chicago: University of Chicago Press, 1948.

Donoghue, Denis, ed. *The Integrity of Yeats.* A series of lectures about Yeats first delivered over Radio Éireann. Cork: Mercier Press for Radio Eireann, 1964.

–––. *William Butler Yeats.* New York: The Viking Press, 1971.

Dunn, Joseph, trans. *The Ancient Irish Epic Tale Tain Bo Cualnge.* London: Nutt, 1914.

Eliade, Mircea. *Images and Symbols.* New York: Sheed and Ward, 1961 (1st French ed., 1952).

Eliot, T. S. "Yeats" (1940). In *On Poetry and Poets.* New York: Farrar, Straus and Cudahy, 1957.

Ellmann, Richard. *The Identity of Yeats.* New York: Oxford University Press, 1964 (1st ed., 1954).

―――. *Yeats: The Man and the Masks.* New York: Dutton-Everyman, 1958 (1st ed., 1948).

Empson, William. *Some Versions of Pastoral.* London: Chatto and Windus, 1935.

Garrab, Arra M. "Fabulous Artifice: Yeats's 'Three Bushes' Sequence," *Criticism,* VIII, iii (Summer, 1965), 235-249.

Graves, Robert. *The White Goddess: A Historical Grammar of Poetic Myth* New York: Noonday, 1966 (1st ed., 1948; 1st American ed., amended, 1966).

Gregory, Lady Augusta. *A Book of Saints and Wonders.* London: John Murray, 1908.

―――. *Poets and Dreamers.* London: John Murray, 1902.

Hall, James, and Martin Steinmann, eds. *The Permanence of Yeats.* New York: Collier, 1961 (1st ed., 1950).

Henn. T. R. *The Lonely Tower.* New York: Pellegrini and Cudahy, 1952.

Hoagland, Kathleen, ed. *1000 Yeats of Irish Poetry.* New York: Grosset and Dunlap, 1962.

Hoare, Dorothy M. *The Works of Morris and of Yeats in Relation to Early Saga Literature.* Cambridge: Cambridge University Press, 1937.

Hone, Joseph. *W. B. Yeats 1865-1939.* New York: St. Martin's Press, 1962.

Hough, Graham. *The Last Romantics.* London: Methuen, 1961 (1st ed., 1947).

Hyde, Douglas. *A Literary History of Ireland from Earliest Times to the Present Day.* London: Fisher Unwin, 1906 (1st ed., 1894).

―――. *The Story of Early Gaelic Literature.* London: Fisher Unwin, 1906. (1st ed., 1894).

Jeffares, A. Norman. *The Poetry of W. B. Yeats.* London: Edward Arnold, 1961.

―――. *W. B. Yeats: Man and Poet* (with corrections). London: Routledge, 1962.

―――. *W. B. Yeats: The Poems.* London: Edward Arnold, 1964.

Kermode, Frank. *Romantic Image.* New York: Vintage, 1964 (1st ed., 1957).

Kirby, Sheelah, comp.; Patrick Gallagher, ed. *The Yeats Country: A Guide to Places in the West of Ireland Associated with the Life and Writings of William Butler Yeats.* Dublin: Dolmen Press, 1965.

The Larousse Encyclopedia of Mythology. London: Paul Hamlyn, 1959.

Lincoln, Eleanor Terry, ed. *Pastoral and Romance: Modern Essays in Criticism.* Englewood Cliffs, N. J.: Prentice-Hall, 1969.

McAlindon, T. "Yeats and the Irish Renaissance," *PMLA*, LXXXII, ii (May, 1967), 157–169.

MacDermott, Martin, ed. *The New Spirit of the Nation; or, Ballads and Songs by the Writers of "The Nation."* London: Fisher Unwin, 1894.

–––. *Songs and Ballads of Young Ireland.* London: Downey and Company, 1896.

MacLeish, Archibald. *Yeats and the Belief in Life.* An address at the University of New Hampshire, Jan. 1957. Durham, N. H.: 1958.

MacLiammóir, Micheál, and Eavan Boland. *W. B. Yeats and His World.* London: Thames and Hudson, 1971.

MacNeice, Louis. *The Poetry of W. B. Yeats.* London: Oxford University Press, 1941.

Marx, Leo. *The Machine in the Garden: Technology and the Pastoral Ideal in America.* Oxford: Oxford University Press, 1967 (1st ed., 1964).

Menon, V. K. Narayana. *The Development of William Butler Yeats.* Preface by Sir Herbert J. C. Grierson. Edinburgh and London: Oliver and Boyd, 1942.

Montgomery, Henry R. *Specimens of the Early Native Poetry of Ireland.* Dublin: Hodges, Figgis, 1892.

Moore, Virginia. *The Unicorn: William Butler Yeats' Search for Reality.* New York: Macmillan, 1954.

Morris, William. *The Earthly Paradise.* 2 vols. London: Longmans, Green, 1896.

–––. *The Well at the World's End (The Collected Works of William Morris,* vols. 18–19). London: Longmans, Green, 1903.

Murphy, Gerard. *Saga and Myth in Ancient Ireland.* Published for the Cultural Relations Committee of Ireland by Colm O Lochlainn. Dublin: Sign of the Three Candles, 1961.

Nathan, Leonard E. *The Tragic Drama of William Butler Yeats: Figures in a Dance.* New York: Columbia University Press, 1965.

Ó Duilearga, ed. *Irish Folk-Tales.* Collected by Jeremiah Curtin. Dublin: Talbot, 1956.

O'Faolain, Eileen. *Irish Saga and Folk-Tales.* London: Oxford University Press, 1963.

O'Grady, Standish. *Selected Essays and Passages.* Dublin: Talbot, n.d.

O'Sullivan, Donal. *Irish Folk Music and Song.* Published for the Cultural Relations Committee of Ireland by Colm O Lochlainn. Dublin: Sign of the Three Candles, 1961.

Parkinson, Thomas. *W. B. Yeats Self-Critic.* Berkeley and Los Angeles: University of California Press, 1951.

Pater, Walter. *Marius the Epicurean.* New York: Book League of America, 1930.

–––. *Miscellaneous Studies: A Series of Essays.* New York: Macmillan, 1902.

Rajan, Balachandra. *W. B. Yeats: A Critical Introduction.* London: Hutchinson University Library, 1965.

Reid, Forrest. *W. B. Yeats: A Critical Study.* New York: Dodd, Mead, 1915.

Robinson, Herbert, and Knox Wilson. *Myths and Legends of All Nations.* New York: Bantam, 1961.

Robinson, Lennox, ed. *Lady Gregory's Journals 1916-1930.* New York: Macmillan, 1930.

Rolleston, T. W. *Myths and Legends of the Celtic Race.* London: Harrap, 1911.

The Second Book of the Rhymers' Club. London: Elkin Matthews and John Lane, 1894.

Seiden, Morton Irving. *William Butler Yeats: The Poet as Mythmaker 1865-1939.* Lansing: Michigan State University Press, 1962.

Stauffer, Donald A. *The Golden Nightingale: Essays on Some Principles of Poetry in the Lyrics of William Butler Yeats.* New York: Macmillan, 1949.

Stock, A. C. *W. B. Yeats: His Poetry and Thought.* Cambridge: Cambridge University Press, 1964 (1st ed., 1961).

Symons, Arthur. *Studies in Prose and Verse.* London: Dent, [1904].

———. *The Symbolist Movement in Literature.* Intro. by Richard Ellmann. New York: Dutton, 1958 (1st rev. ed., 1919).

Tate, Allen. "Yeats' Romanticism." In Allen Tate, *The Man of Letters in the Modern World: Selected Essays, 1928-1955.* London: Meridian (Thames and Hudson), 1957.

Thurneysen, Rudolf. *Die Irische Helden-und Königsage bis zum Siebzehnten Jahrhundert.* Teile I und II. Halle: Max Niemeyer,1921.

Unterecker, John. *A Reader's Guide to William Butler Yeats.* New York: Noonday Press, 1959.

———. ed., *Yeats: A Collection of Critical Essays.* Englewood Cliffs, N. J.: Prentice-Hall, 1963.

Ure, Peter. *Yeats.* Edinburgh and London: Oliver and Boyd, 1963.

Warren, Austin. "William Butler Yeats: The Religion of a Poet." In Austin Warren, *Rage for Order.* Ann Arbor: University of Michigan Press, 1959.

Wilson, Colin. *The Strength to Dream: Literature and the Imagination.* Boston: Houghton Mifflin, 1962.

Wilson, Edmund. *Axel's Castle: A Study of the Imaginative Literature of 1870-1930.* New York: Scribner's 1931.

Wilson, F. A. C. *W. B. Yeats and Tradition.* New York: Macmillan, 1958.

———. *Yeats's Iconography.* New York: Macmillan, 1960.

Zwerdling, Alex. *Yeats and the Heroic Ideal.* New York: New York University Press, 1965.

INDEX

Abbey Players, The, 17
Anima Mundi, 120
Arcadia, Arcadian, 15, 16, 20, 21,
    60-62, 72, 77-80, 85-87, 93, 105
Arnold, Matthew, 16, 57
Art for Art's Sake, 4, 5
Axel (Villiers de l'Isle-Adam),
    Yeats's comments on, quoted
    9, 116, 121-122, 127

Beckett, Samuel, 4
Beltaine, 36
Ben Bulben, 16
Blake, William, 7, 91, 101, 130
Blavatsky, Madame Helena, 14,
    58, 65
Brendan, Saint, 57, 93
Byzantium (as concept), 103, 124,
    137

Cathleen Ni Houlihan, 35
Celtic Twilight, 8, 24, 31, 39-41,
    54, 97, 105, 130
Chatterjee, Mohini, 14
Comyn, Michael (as source), 91
Coole Park, 17, 99

Danaan, Tuatha de Danaan (see
    also Fairy, Sidhe), 13, 94, 136
Drama (as poetry), 12
Dromohair, 16, 21

Druid, Druids, Druidism, 12-15,
    27, 38, 47-50, 65-69,
    104-107, 115, 123
Dublin, 19

Eliot, T. S., 43
Experimental writing, 4

Fairy, Fairies, fairyland, faerie,
    etc. (see also Danaan, Tuatha
    de Danaan, Sidhe), 11, 16, 20,
    21, 42-45, 50, 56, 60, 68, 86,
    104-106, 111
Faulkner, William, 5

Gaelic (and Yeats), 5, 131
Galway, 10, 15
Gonne, Maud, 8, 17, 36, 110
Gregory, Lady Augusta, 13

Hardy, Thomas, 43
Hellas (Shelley), 58
Heraclitus, 47
Hermetical Society of the Golden
    Dawn, The, 7, 98
Homer, 4
Hyde, Douglas, 65-66

Impermanence, 5
India, Indian, 15, 16, 20, 21, 72,
    79-87, 93, 105